Man in Motion

Alexander Thomas

This edition was published by The Dreamwork Collective
The Dreamwork Collective LLC, Dubai, United Arab Emirates
thedreamworkcollective.com
Printed and bound in the United Arab Emirates
Cover and design: Nuno Moreira, NMDESIGN.ORG
Text © Alexander Thomas
ISBN: 978-9948-8719-7-2
Approved by National Media Council Dubai, United Arab Emirates
MC-02-01-3054113

Man in Motion

A SUBURBAN

TECH GUY'S

JOURNEY

INTO LOVE

AND WISDOM

Alexander Thomas

To Ketra and Ralph, for the spark.

To Mike and Mohammed, pillars in the temple of manhood.

To Emma, Jesse, Amelia, and Elliott, you fill up my cup.

And Nancy...

"Anyone who has seen her smile has known perfection. She instills grace in every common thing and divinity in every careless gesture."

— Edmond Rostand, *Cyrano de Bergerac*

Robert & Thérèse Sauriol - In Memoriam.

In the desert city of Dubai, there is a road. Beside the road is a canal. The sun is setting, orange hues and persimmon. There's an old man ambling into view. Leathered face, grey beard. The day's heat has subsided and there is a warm, wet breeze. The old man walks slowly along the canal. He pauses and looks toward the dhows, the Arabian sailboats from a bygone era.

In the city, the old man seems wayward, like a shepherd without a flock. A Bedouin, silky white robe and head wrapped in a keffiyeh. He wanders, and from across the road, I wonder. I imagine a past or maybe a future: camels and caravans under a crescent moon; a fire that crackles and spits into a clear Arabian night. And beyond the night the cosmos swirls, Aquila soars and Andromeda shimmers. In this dream, the old man moves with poise and purpose.

I imagine him over beyond the dunes, warming by a fire in the cool desert night. The old nomad feeding the flames with small branches and dry logs while an old woman sits watching. See her now: body covered by a black madraga, face withered and faded by time but eyes noble and knowing. Her grace pulls me in. I take my place beside her and we gaze. At the fire and at the sky above. The stars shine bright and the cosmos is in motion. The slow rhythm. The eternal underlying cadence of all things.

The fire radiates; warmth pushing against the cold night air. The old woman removes a small pouch from her satchel and passes it to the old man. He walks toward the silhouette of a camel. He touches his forehead to the animal's mouth and opens the ragged cloth full of seeds and dried leaves. She looks on as the camel feeds from his hand. Above us a shooting star, a streak of light, disappearing into inky blackness. She nudges me to look up again. She stretches her arm upward; she points a bent finger toward the constellation of Orion and a red-orange star, Betelgeuse.

The old man makes his way back to her. He stands in place and looks down at her. His arms rock gently. He hums under his breath. His feet rising slowly and falling softly. She smiles. He is dancing. The slow rhythm. Smoke rising behind him, his face glows iridescent, shades of earth and fire. He is smiling. He is looking into her eyes. She is looking into his. He offers her his hands and pulls her up. She rises to him gently and they dance. She looks away from him, toward me. She glares fiercely into my eyes. She nods, recognizing that I understand. She approaches me. Places her hands around my cheeks and kisses my forehead. He bends over and picks up the last dry log and hands it to me. He looks at her again, with admiration and pride. He moves his hand to hers and clasps it. Their hands interlocked, they walk into the night, into the desert. They walk, hand in hand, and vanish over the dunes and into the dark.

Beside me, the camel stands tall. I smile. The camel looks to the side and spits. We have work to do. I put the log on the fire and bend my knee to the ground. I bow my head and whisper. Thank you.

Part I – The Priest

The old man spoke only once, through a dream. And he said only this:

Let God go.

INTRODUCTION — SPIRITUALLY CURIOUS

Dubai, UAE: Spring 2020

The world circa Spring 2020 is at the beginning stages of a global pandemic. Tensions between global powers are rising in the South China Sea. Trust in Western democratic institutions is declining rapidly. The airwaves are saturated with hostility and confusion. My family is fractured, separated by land and sea. I have become nomadic. Without a community or home, I wander. My body is in Dubai but my consciousness is outside time, floating in the warm ethereal waters of eternity. Here I can relive moments past and glimpse unimagined futures. I am not in control; the reveries come along like waves that I surf with curiosity and compassion, joy and wonder. Since the shamanic ceremony, I have not been fully put back together. I have not reintegrated my awareness into my body's time and place. I am outside myself while life beckons, a siren's call on a distant shore, to be fully realized and attached. To care about the world of time again. To love.

Inside time, my body is anxious. Full of worry. View from the balcony:

South is the Arabian Sea, hues of blue and green by day but now, before sunrise, it is featureless and grey. Southeast, a mostly empty contemporary condo complex; eight stories of glass, steel, and white fascia. Most of the tenants left before the lockdown started. Southwest, an industrial coastline. Energy plants and aluminum factories. Banks of cranes and exhaust stacks. Blinking red lights and a lone narrow fire atop a tall pipe.

I've been up since 2 a.m. There was a storm. I heard the thunder but did not see the lightning. It passed. It's still dark and I'm already three coffees into the day. The birds are only now starting to wake up and chirp. Since the quarantine started, this balcony has become a nut and berry buffet for at least a dozen different birds. Mostly the myna but I've seen a crow and a sparrow. It's warm. The air is thick with humidity. It's not yet desert hot but the signs are there. I'm already starting to sweat and the sun's not fully risen.

I'm chatting with Mike over WhatsApp. It's late evening in North America.

"Alex, it's snowing here!! How is Dubai?" he asks.

"Mike! I'm in exile and under house arrest, how are you guys doing?" I ask.

"Anne and I have been up and down. I've been generally prickly for the better part of three months and this additional anxiety over the pandemic hasn't helped. All four boys are stuck inside with us—

driving me bananas. Lost my shit on them a few times. Anne told me to give it a rest."

"Saint Anne," I say.

"How's your business? Are you under any pressure?" he asks.

"Are you asking if my aviation technology company is affected by a global aviation shutdown, economic collapse, and the threat of war in the Gulf and South China Sea?"

"Don't be an ass!"

"Shareholders asked us to build a couple of scenarios: cost of bankruptcy versus cost of a skeleton crew," I tell him.

"That's a lot of pressure," he replies.

"Not really. Strangely enough, I haven't felt this free and calm in twenty years."

"Now I'm curious," he says.

"Man, there are wealthy guys who basically own countries that are worried. Let them figure it out. In the meantime, I'm going to catch up on some reading and learning how to yoga."

"I really don't believe you. It's early over there, you've probably been up worrying all night," he says, "Any chance you'll need to move back?"

"Who knows, Mike. This morning I tried praying… just to be able to see my kids again one more time."

"You will see them again."

We end our chat with Mike having the last word. I hate it when he does that. He's one of my best friends, but sometimes, when I share the way I'm feeling about something, I just want to be heard.

Mike offering a fact-free opinion when I'm sharing a feeling reminds me of the thousands of times I've done the same thing to people around me. I'm a terrible listener but I'm striving to be better. I tend to think more than feel. I'm 60 percent nerd, roughly. I push hard to get that down below 50 percent. Less than half nerd so I can be tolerable in a relationship. It's not easy.

Of course, I woke up worried I might never see my kids again. I promised them I'd be home every Christmas and summer. I didn't factor in a global aviation collapse and whatever is to come. I've never been in a pandemic before, but the world feels a little apocalyptic right now. I've never been in an apocalypse either, so yeah, *I'm a little worried, Mike.*

The Germans have a word that the English borrowed: zeitgeist, the spirit of our times. We are living in a period of unprecedented power and ignorance in equal measure. We are the generation that has all but succeeded in conquering the natural world, and not a single person alive has a reasonable clue as to why. Why we run, why we conquer. Great power and a great deal more confusion, the thematic undertone of our zeitgeist.

My grandad used to say that an ignorant man speaking his ignorance is just an ignorant man, leave him alone. An ignorant man speaking his ignorance passionately, well that right there is a fool. Try and not become one of those.

I've spoken my ignorance passionately more than once. I strive to do that a little less now. But *these times*. These times feel like there are a lot of people speaking and acting passionately on their ignorance. This wouldn't be so much of an issue but for the nuclear weapons they control, the havoc being wreaked on our shared ecosystem, and the generational disenfranchisement, oppression, and outright enslavement that still happens in 2020.

I also woke up a little sad. That I'll never walk my girls down the aisle or have some guy time with my son. That I won't ever be a grandad. It's just a feeling. Not a strong feeling, as in any kind of imminent threat; it's just a new possibility that these times have brought, something that I had never really considered before.

Here in Dubai, whenever you make plans with someone, they always say *Inshallah*. God willing.

I will see the kids again, *Inshallah*.

The times are strange. Tragic for a lot of people, but so far for me, just surreal. Generally, I'm a pretty rational guy, but there's a dreamlike texture to my world now. The news reports are pulling at the fabric of my reality. Leaders around the world have taken on a mildly cartoonlike quality. And I live in a Middle-Eastern desert, thousands of miles from the snowy valley I grew up in. Thinking about it this morning, it's been an adventure since I visited Maui with my friend Fadi a few years ago.

My circle of manhood is pretty tight. Mike is my rock. A few years older than me and stoic, unchanging. Fadi is a buccaneer and a few years younger than me. My brothers-in-arms. They've been beside me these past seven years in my search for a kind of truth. For wisdom, for some way of calibrating my internal compass with the world around me. True North.

I don't have answers, but I'm sharing my journey through my own ignorance toward a kind of goodness that I can live with.

I haven't been a particularly religious person. Born and raised Catholic. Spent a little time as an altar boy. Nothing negative to report there but I left the Church in my teens because it didn't feel religious to me then. The experience all felt very... political. In my twenties, an atheist, closed minded to any and all possibilities. As a young dad, agnostic. Neither for nor against any particular religion or conceptualization of God.

Then spiritually curious. Mildly Buddhist with a dash of New Testament. This God stuff, *what is really going on there?* There's something in there I've always wanted to understand. What were all those people really talking about? And just before the pandemic kicked in, I met a shaman and participated in a mystical ceremony. That's when things got really weird.

Today, if I had to label it, omni-religious. If it wasn't for the quarantine, I would have visited Nepal last month for a Hindu celebration of Lord Shiva, one of the many religious figures in India and parts of the Himalayas. I wanted to visit the sadhus. The bizarre, ash-covered holy men of India and Nepal. As I write this here in Dubai, we are only a few days away from Ramadan. A period of fasting, charity, and devotion to community between lunar cycles. As a guest in a foreign country, I do my best to respect the tradition and I observe with fascination.

There's another reason my compass is spinning: I have a penis. Testicles also.

I once overheard an old man ask a plumber friend of mine for a new toilet. One with a higher seat. "But you're in great shape. Why do you need a handicapped toilet?" my friend asked. "Because every time I sit down my testicles get wet!" said the old man.

That about sums up how I used to think of manhood. A young man fumbles his way through life trying to make babies, a man tries to raise babies, and an old man tries to hold on to his comfort and keep his testicles dry. I know a little more about manhood today than when I started the journey, but I'm still learning.

Last thing: My skin is fair. My eyes are blue. I made more money than anyone I knew growing up. I have a few watches that are worth more than every car my dad ever owned. I've travelled around the world for a technology business I started. About all of this, I feel neither guilt nor pride. It just is what it is. Most of my life has been reactive.

I was shot out of the womb a little over forty-five years ago into a world of people who were running. I ran along with them. I ran as far as I could as fast as I could. I left people behind, I pushed people out of my way, I leapt over the injured and the sick. I admired those who could run faster. I held veiled contempt for those who couldn't keep up. *We have to outrun the wolves; I'll worry about where I'm going once I get there.*

To my peers in business, I look like a normal guy. I wear nice suits. I strike all the right notes when I speak. My LinkedIn profile has just the right amount of normal, wealth-building capitalist on the page. I fly around the world. I sit in boardrooms. *Normal.* To my kids, friends, and family, I'm a stand-up guy. I meet all my obligations and live up to my responsibilities. But inside. Inside I'm spinning. *I know what I'm doing. I just don't know why I'm doing it.*

The closest thing to north on my compass was my paternal grandad. When he passed, my world fell apart. I once hoped to be able to carry his values of family, community, and the Church forward in my own life. My life was going to be a straight line, from him to me and on to my son.

Today, I'm something else. A nomad in the desert searching for his tribe. Or just a nerd trapped on his balcony with a couple of Indian pigeons, breathing into the transformation of the world.

CHAPTER 1 — VIGIL

The difference between a boy and a man isn't in how he looks but in what he knows to be true. It's in how he lives and how he loves. It's in his confidence, deeply rooted in nature's bounty—the gift of his own life. I am reliving these fragments of memory with newfound compassion. A love and understanding in the heart of the man I am today for the boy that I was only a few years ago. If I could send a message through time, I would tell that boy only this: It's going to be okay, let go, relax into it, trust that the arc of Life bends toward goodness, and when you can, try, just try and be a little kinder.

Seven years before the global pandemic.

The body on the hospice bed is a breathing husk of a once-great man. The wisest man I knew.

I am alone with him. Called here earlier this morning by his doctor and warned that today, my grandfather would draw his last breath. My dad is here and so are his sisters, my aunts. But they aren't in the room. They are in the halls or coffee shop. Their vigil has lasted weeks, mine only a few hours. I will not leave this room. I am a sentinel to this moment.

The room is lit by the winter sun. There are trinkets on the shelf. Photos of family, grandkids, newspaper articles. Old postcards and needlepoint artwork, created by his hands to pass the time in these last few years.

He lies unconscious. Breathing, barely. Occasionally, seconds pass between rasps. Each time I wonder: *Is this it? The last and final breath?* For over ninety years he breathed. For over sixty of those he loved the same woman. She's a few rooms over, on the same floor. She has no conscious idea that today will be his last. That's a blessing. Their love never fizzled. No sharp stings of pain or loss. No anguish, just sleep. Breathing gently into the goodnight.

My last memory of their years together was at the cottage. Just before dinner. She sat in a chair, head tilted back while he stood over her with eye drops, gently, tenderly squeezing out each drop into each of her eyes. She never blinked. Absolute trust. The two were indeed one.

She did, however, throw a potato at him once; he made the mistake of saying he wasn't hungry after she cooked a meal for them. To be clear, there were peaks and troughs in that marriage, but the blessing is this: She will never feel the pain of life without him, and nor will he feel the pain of life without her.

For almost forty of his years, I was his namesake. The firstborn son to the firstborn son. We are far from royalty, and to most people, namesakes don't mean much of anything. But to my grandad and me, it was a secret handshake. A wink. A knowing and a responsibility— for him to teach and for me to learn. Work hard, be responsible, and take care of your family. Dress up on Sundays, go to church, help your community. Be generous and love until it hurts then just keep on loving. And family. Family is *everything*.

My dad peeks his head into the room.

"Still breathing?" he asks. My dad is addled. It's been his general state of being for the past decade or so. Forlorn and confused. He's made this day about himself, another terrible day in his life full of woe and suffering. He walks over to the bedside, mumbles a few words, cries a little and leaves.

The pauses between breaths are getting longer.

If I revere my grandad as a man, I resent my dad for the same reasons. Where my grandad was strong, my dad was weak. Where my grandad was selfless and cared for his community, my dad was self-centred and couldn't even take care of himself. He broke my mom's heart. Time after time he broke her heart.

Work was his mistress. Glory and power. Always working, driving. Never there for her when she needed him. And when the career sputtered, the drugs started. Sleep medication. Pain medication. Disability insurance and muscle relaxants. A twenty-first-century cocktail of barbiturates, loathing, opiates, and fear.

I avoid talking to my dad as much as I can and focus on my grandad. I stand over him. I watch. I wait for the final moment. The lump in my throat grows.

I'm not crying. It's something I try to avoid at all costs. Whenever I feel a tear brewing, I start chewing the inside of my cheek. Small stings. The tears abate. I move closer to the bedside to stroke his hair and chew my cheek.

A few years ago, I was in the emergency room with my grandad. He was sitting up on the bed that time, though. His shirt was off. Gauze and tape all over his torso. Small scratches and red dots on his skin. He had just finished trying to kill himself with a dull kitchen knife when one of my aunts called me.

"I couldn't take her pain anymore," he said.

"She hurt her hip. She was in so much pain. She couldn't walk. She couldn't sleep. She was in agony. She moaned all night. I couldn't do anything. I tried looking for something sharp to put through my heart. It hurt too much. I tried finding a place where it wouldn't hurt... it hurt too much everywhere," he said and bowed his head.

"Every morning I pray. Every morning I pray to the little Jesus on my dresser. 'Please take me... my bags are packed... you have given me so much... so much, but please just one last thing... take me home.' Every morning I pray," he said, trailing off and looking down at the floor.

I could do nothing for him but listen. And watch as the doctors and my aunts fretted about his sanity. Watch as the medication piled up and watch the man disappear slowly. His wit and vitality dulled and stupefied. His tender and passionate heart washed over by waves of SSRIs. He loved her until it hurt, and then kept on loving until the very end.

In the room with him now, I stroke his hair and chew my cheek.

And then I stop.

Something happened at the instant of the last exhale. I feel it before I see it. I am alone in the room. He's gone and I suddenly feel so incredibly inadequate. So unprepared. That I have failed to become even a fraction of the man he was. I'm not ready for life without his guidance.

He was the last of a long line of strong and wise men that had passed through my life. And now I feel so totally and completely alone, without strength or wisdom to navigate my way. The chief of my tribe, the stoic face on the top of my tribal totem pole. Gone.

"If somehow you can still hear me. Please... Please keep showing me the way. I don't know what to do anymore," I whisper into the silence.

My dad looks into the room. I look toward him and nod.

"Oh no!" He rushes to the bedside. "I love you, Papa, I love you," he says through tears.

My aunts soon join him. They hold hands together and speak words of love. Prayers and tears. My grandad is gone. I stand back and watch. I stretch the moment out to be in his presence as long as I can. My dad and his sisters, holding hands around a hospital bed. I nod to them quietly before leaving. Walking out, I check my phone.

Missed calls. Messages. Kids. Wife. Work. Emails and texts. Things are a little tense at home.

In the hallway, a nurse stops me. "That was your grandfather?" she asks.

"Yes," I say.

"Here." She hands me a wallet-size photo.

It's not a great picture. His eyes were closed and he was long past his prime. He had been in the hospice for the past five years. But she had kept it; my grandad meant something to this young woman and now she was passing the picture on to me.

"He was a good man," she says.

I thank her and walk briskly to the elevator. I rush out the front doors of the hospital into the freezing car. I leave the engine off and weep. Alone, I can cry. I cry until the tears run dry. It's out of my system. Calls need to be made.

CHAPTER 2 — WHEN THE CENTRE DOESN'T HOLD

I'm sitting on Mike's front porch. Just Mike and I. Our families are out back enjoying the pool.

I'm a little emotional and doing my best to keep it together.

We buried my grandad a few months ago. The church was full. The man had been retired for thirty years but I was amazed at how many former employees came to me and shook my hand. He was an assistant manager at the local grocery store. He never became a full manager because, at the time, the most senior positions were reserved for native English. My grandad was a proud French Canadian in an era of open discrimination against people who spoke the way he did.

"Have you started eating yet?" Mike asks.

"No. Still just peanut butter," I answer.

"You have to start eating, man," he says.

I haven't eaten anything other than peanut butter for weeks. I have no appetite for anything else. I started smoking again. I feel like I've mourned my grandad well enough. Business is going great. I sold some shares in my company, paid off the mortgage, renovated the house. I am literally living in my dream home. I built some shutters out of poplar that are stunning. The kids are healthy, and we have a mix of bamboo flooring and Berber carpet. Apart from my wife wanting to split up, things are really good.

"Have you guys made a decision?" he wonders.

"One day at a time, man," I reply. "I don't know. Sometimes I think she's going to stay. I have hope. Most days I don't."

He puts his big hand on my shoulder, and I start chewing the inside of my cheek. Mike and I met through some mutual friends at a men's spiritual retreat. It was my first one. It's a little embarrassing to admit this now, but I had read that the spiritual life could help me make more money. Law of Attraction and whatnot.

The retreat was at a convent. I remember Mike then, sitting at a table. A few other men sitting beside us in the cafeteria. There was a table full of nuns not too far away. The men were wearing pyjamas or jogging pants. It was a relaxed, fraternal bonding kind of weekend. Sessions with a priest-facilitator to open the men up to the inner life. Card games, cafeteria food, and conversations in between.

Mike was telling the table a story. Commanding the room. There was power in his telling. The men were transfixed.

"I hired a guy once. He was always late," he started.

"The guy had the worst kind of luck you could possibly imagine. Something happened when he was really young. It was a strange and tragic thing. The kid was playing outside with his sister and he threw something at her. Was a small rock... a pebble or something. Was more playful than mean."

"Something happens to her. It had nothing to do with the rock. She has some kind of internal malfunction. Whatever the kid version of a stroke is. She dies. Parents are devastated. They explain to the kid it wasn't his fault, but something breaks inside him too. That's real tragedy."

"Years later, he marries this lady. She cheats on him. All the time. He catches her. She tells him it's over. On they go. She gets pregnant. Has the baby. Kid is clearly not his. As in totally different race. She tells him it was just that one time. He forgives her, raises the kid as his own. Comes home one day, she's being filmed. Couple of guys naked along with her. She's recording a fucking porno. He confronts her. She leaves. She leaves him and the kid and he never hears from her again."

"Few more years go by, he meets another lady. They fall in love. She has two kids. He's got the one. They move in together. Life is beautiful. Until it's not. She gets breast cancer. She dies and leaves him the kids. He's raising three kids on his own and is always late because he's always dealing with one thing or another." Mike finishes the story. Around the table, a look of incredulity on all the men's faces.

"So what happened?" I asked.

"I fired him. I can't deal with someone who's always late," he said.

The men at the table roared with laughter. Gallows humour in a convent.

I doubt it's a true story but at a table full of strong men, Mike commands attention. If the story is true, and Mike did fire the guy, knowing him like I do he's probably sending the guy money every month and paying for the kids' education. Mike runs his business with integrity; he owes that to the people who work for him and he owes it to his customers. But Mike is also incredibly generous and loving.

He's been calling me daily since my marriage started to unravel. Unravel might be generous. The new therapy narrative is that there was never any love to begin with. I don't know about any of that, I just know that, right now, I'm a little bewildered. *I don't understand… but we just put in new carpets?*

I probably went two decades without shedding a tear, but the last few months: waterworks and bloody cheeks. I've managed to keep the crying to the moments when I'm alone, but now with Mike, I'm a wet mess.

The pain is a weight I can't get rid of. Every minute of every day, I'm carrying it. Doesn't matter who I'm with or what I'm doing, I have my arms wrapped around a big, heavy, sharp, and awkward stone of pain. When Mike puts his hand on my shoulder or calls me before starting his day, he helps me carry the rock for a little while and that's why I'm crying. Tears of gratitude.

Whatever else this mess has brought me, the tenderness and love of my closest of friends is a blessing.

"Try eating a little, man. You look like a ghost," he coaxes.

"Fuck off, Mike."

#

All three kids are sitting around the kitchen island. It's an early dinner before Jesse's hockey. Amelia, the youngest, sits between Jesse and Emma, my eldest. They are twelve, ten, and nine. Rosy cheeks and painted-on moustaches. It's the last day of Movember. An event where men grow moustaches in support of cancer.

My wife is behind the counter. She's oddly eager to give them the news now. At first, she wanted to wait until after Christmas, but that didn't feel right to me. I've always tried to be honest with the kids, warts and all. I wanted to tell them the moment the decision was made, and we pretty much did.

I'm watching in stunned silence because my life is unravelling, and fast.

"Your dad and I have some news," she says.

In unison, they stop eating and look up at her with anticipation.

"We've decided to get a divorce," she tells them.

She's happy. She tries hard to mask it, but she's happy. For her, it's a moment of liberation and exhilaration. For me, it's pain and fear. Logistics and lawyers, accountants and new problems that she'll never have to worry about. It's all just going to happen, the infrastructure tearing itself apart and rebuilding without impacting her service delivery.

And failure. In the model of the world my grandad taught me, it is the most grievous kind of failure a man could succumb to. Failure to keep the family together.

The moment is suspended in time, like an odd contemporary painting: three children around a kitchen island with drawn-on moustaches; looks of profound confusion, surprise, delight, and utter devastation. A great building, one that had withstood the test of their entire time, was collapsing in front of their eyes while someone danced a jig in the foreground. She's had plenty of great moments as a mom, but this isn't one of them.

It's silent. They look at me, stunned. I don't know what to say. They never saw it coming. There was no fighting or screaming; it wasn't that kind of marriage. It's been months of counselling. What I thought was marriage therapy was actually more like grief counselling. The decision had been made. I had been brought gently through the stages of letting go. From denial through to painful acceptance. Family, as I understood it, was no more.

The kids are looking at me and I don't have the faintest idea about anything. My world is now officially upside down.

"Are we still going to Jesse's hockey?" Emma asks.

"We sure are," my wife—ex-wife—says. "Things are going to be as normal as possible. We can talk more in the car ride over."

I see Jesse's shoulders sag. His expression is stoic, but his strength has been sapped, and his body can't support the weight of his shoulders.

I know what to do now.

I pick him up and hold him tight. His body goes limp in my arms.

"We're not going to go to hockey tonight, Bud," I whisper in his ear.

And he starts to cry. I haven't seen him cry since he was a baby. I carry him in my arms toward the front door. I grab his jacket. "Dad's going to take you guys for a drive," I say to the girls.

"I'm just taking them for some ice cream," I tell their mom.

"It's winter," she says.

I don't answer. I don't need to answer anymore.

#

It's Christmas Eve. I've packed my bag and left my old home. My new house won't be ready for a few more weeks so I'm officially homeless. I have a car, a credit card, a backpack, and a book. And I'm in the parking lot of a Best Buy. I just finished dinner in a pizza joint nearby. Alone, I toyed with a plate full of food, stretching the time out as long as I could. Fadi, my new roommate, is coming back from a party in a few hours and I don't yet have a key to his place.

It's cold. The air doesn't usually get this frigid until late January. I sit in the car with the engine running, the heating turned up.

Jesse had hockey earlier. Early Christmas Eve game, the last game before the break. The arena was packed. The boys won. The arena was so warm. Everyone was happy, and for a moment, so was I. Emma and Amelia sat with me.

After Jesse came out, I hugged him and walked him and the girls outside to their mom's car. I wished them a merry Christmas. I would be seeing them tomorrow, but not spending Christmas Eve with them seemed like a major life event. I said goodbye like I was leaving the country. And now, looking up at the bright yellow Best Buy sign and the last-minute shoppers, I decide to head into the store. I have nothing to buy, but I just don't want to be alone in the car.

If there is such a thing as an exact opposite to midnight mass with family, it's this Best Buy on this Christmas Eve. Fluorescent lighting and dirty floors. Red and green foil tinsel sagging on the walls and strewn in the aisles. Bored young clerks and hurried shoppers. I pretend to look for something. I walk slowly. Browsing. Every aisle. Slowly. I want to stay warm and be near people. But I don't want to be weird. My browsing isn't quite so aimless. I try and get as close to people as I can without making anyone uncomfortable.

Staying warm and not being alone on Christmas Eve. That's the extent of my new life plan.

I call Fadi. No answer. Hopefully he's driving.

We've worked together for almost ten years. He was employee number five in a company I started. We travelled the world together, selling new technology to airports. We've become very close. Like brothers. He's recently divorced. Six months ago, I was giving him marital advice. Hubris. Now he's giving me dating advice.

My phone rings. It's Fadi, finally.

"What are you up to?" he asks.

"Hanging out at Best Buy just waiting for your call," I say.

"I'm leaving in five. Meet at my place in an hour?" he says.

I walk back to the car and turn the engine on to stay warm. I've been trying to avoid quiet time these past few months. Those moments where I have time to think and feel. If I look forward, I see a bleak future. If I look backward, I feel regret. The here and now is cold and miserable.

It was a no-fault divorce. Thirteen years of marriage and twenty years of knowing each other, a fatigue crept in. Accumulation of injuries. Petty and careless moments. Nothing to be ashamed of, just stuff to regret.

I worked. Since I was twelve, I worked. In my twenties it was almost all I cared about. More money faster. I reached my financial goal before I was thirty-five. By then the goal didn't matter. I paid the house off, the cars got upgraded, the vacations got more exotic. I wanted more. Faster. I was competitive. I wanted to win a race. A lot of life gets missed between the calls and the emails.

Alone in a cold car on Christmas Eve. *Congratulations, bro. You won.*

#

I slowly drive to Fadi's place and wait for him in the car. I haven't seen his place yet. He's been telling me about the renovations. I see the garage door start to open before I see his headlights.

Inside is more construction site than house. Plastic tarps over kitchen cupboards. Drywall dust on every surface. Fadi is wearing a cap and a leather jacket. Mid-thirties, handsome. Olive skin, dark hair, and a bright smile. He's a happy guy. Extroverted. Loves meeting new people and watching home renovation programs on TV.

"Sorry, man, things are still a little chaotic here," he says.

"It's all good, brother, just grateful you could accommodate me until the house is ready," I say.

"I bought you an air mattress," he says.

"Oh, okay, great," I say, trying to sound grateful. Fadi went out of his way in a busy period of his life to get me an air mattress. Deep down, I know this is something I should be thankful for, but that well is pretty dry right now.

I feel a surge of anger well up. I think about my to-do list. My shit-list. I forgot about the new mattresses. I had just bought a new mattress for the house I used to own. Fuck. I have to buy a new one. Four new ones for the new place. It hits me. I now need a new ironing board, pots, pans. Shitty IKEA furniture for the kids' rooms. New snowblower, shovels, lawnmower, TVs, couches. I hate shopping. My ex-wife stopped working. She wants to be a student. Start over again. I have to fill two pantries and fridges. Two gas tanks. Two lots of electricity and heating bills. I've already started paying for two lawyers to argue with each other.

Fadi shows me to my bedroom. It's bare, except for the dusty air mattress in the middle of it.

"Sorry, I don't have any sheets but I bought you a sleeping bag," he says.

"Thanks, man," I say.

Again, I try to be grateful. Fadi came back early from a party he'd still be at if it wasn't for me. I'm trying and failing. I'm oscillating between rage and despair. He bought the cheapest sleeping bag he could find. Some kind of polyester on the inside that won't breathe. I'm going to sweat and stink all night. *Fuck you, Fadi.*

"What's the book?" Fadi asks.

"Hard to explain, but mainly it's about love," I say. Since the spiritual retreat five years ago, I've been doing a little exploring. The inner life. I was opening up. Less certainty about the way the world was or wasn't. My atheism shifted toward agnosticism. Today, maybe even a little curiosity around mysticism. The book is about love. Over a thousand pages. I'm not even sure how I came across it, but right now I cling to it like a drowning man holds on to a buoy.

"Can you summarize it?"

Damn it, Fadi. Always looking for the Cliff Notes. Fadi is one of the only people I can talk to about the inner life. I usually love exploring the mystics with him, the deeper wisdom and truths about life, the source of life, life beyond death. I like reading the source material, the raw research, the books the teachers read, not so much the book any one institution or organization recommends.

Our conversations are usually exploratory and at least for me, revealing. Never conclusive. Just a slow walk through the great mysteries and mystics. He asks interesting questions. I attempt to distill or point to some interesting spiritual concept that I'm trying to put into practice. We both, maybe, get a little wiser, a little more compassionate. At the very least the conversations are enjoyable. Usually.

But I don't want to engage, not tonight.

"Fadi, it's over a thousand pages."

"But you only brought one book. Why that one?"

"Because I'm trying to love. It's a book about forgiveness. About innocence. I don't want to be bitter and that's a hard thing for me. This whole deal is fucked but maybe it doesn't have to be. I want to be the most generous and loving person I can be regardless of what's happening around me. But I don't know how to do that because, honestly, right now I just want the world to burn because that's how I feel inside."

"Is it any good?"

"I don't know, man. I'm only halfway through. It's a tough read."

"But what is it saying?"

"Fadi, I'm going to get some sleep. It's been a long day. If you want you can take it and read it tonight."

"Okay, man. It's okay. I just wanted to chat. By the way, I don't have a coffee maker for tomorrow morning. I usually just grab one from Starbucks."

Fuck. No morning coffee. Merry Christmas.

I can't put into practice any insight that I've gleaned from the book. The ability to be totally present with people. To be loving in the present tense. To pay attention. To be fearless and free. There's a story I've just read about Jesus. The man is getting nailed to a cross but somehow is present to the suffering, the feelings of guilt and confusion that the soldier with the hammer is feeling. He feels love and connection with the man hurting him. He sees through the pain of his own body to the pain in the soldier's heart. He says something to soothe any guilt the soldier might feel.

I liked the story but right now I can't even find my way past seething, never mind soothing. *How the fuck could Fadi not have a coffee maker?*

CHAPTER 3 — SNOW DAY

We moved into the new house and got a dog. The kids always wanted a dog. These days I'm a little manic. I'll do just about anything if I think it'll make them smile. I didn't think I was really a dog person before. After getting the beagle, I can confirm that I am definitely not a dog person.

Jesse has on his coat and boots. Theo, the new beagle, is on a leash. They are about to head out for a morning walk. That was the condition: We could get a dog if the kids took turns walking him. We've been housetraining him for a month and still, every day there are accidents.

"Jesse, don't forget the plastic bag," I say.

"It's okay, Pop, I don't need one," he answers and opens the door.

"Hold on, wait, what?" I say.

"Whenever he stops, I tug on the leash. That way he doesn't poop outside on the pavement," he says.

Every day I've been cleaning up one mess after another. Figuratively and literally. Last week I did laundry. Sheets, towels, and three kids' worth of laundry. Six loads in all. The only satisfying thing I can say about laundry is how good the clothes smell when they come out of the dryer. Except last week they didn't. They smelled weird. Not terrible but not good either.

It wasn't until the very last load that I noticed there was a small piece of dog shit wedged into the rubber gasket of the tumbler. Somehow a piece of shit had found its way into the wash and I'd devoted an entire Sunday to reverse washing five loads of wash. Each load, gently infused with the essence of dog shit.

"What the fuck are you talking about?" I exclaim.

I swear at my kids now. I've turned into a guy who swears constantly. I can't go more than a couple of sentences without an expletive of some kind. I've spent the last few years exploring the realms of spirituality, wisdom, and religion, and I can't even speak gently to the people I love the most in my life at the time they need it most.

"I don't want the neighbours to step in poop," he says.

"That's what the fucking bag is for! What is wrong with you?" I shout.

"Why are you screaming?" he asks.

"Because for a month you've been reverse training the god damn dog! You've taught him that it's better to shit inside than outside. Jesus!" I answer.

And then I hug him. From anxiety to rage to remorse in less than a minute.

"Buddy, I'm sorry. It's just that if we don't train him now, while he's young, he'll never really get it. I'm sorry for screaming and swearing."

All my emotions are close to the surface. I'm running hot and I oscillate from one extreme to another. The kids are here for a week, then with their mom for a week. The off weeks are the worst. I can't get over the feeling of not being around them. The house is so empty. I sleep. Catch up on chores. I try watching TV but can't concentrate.

The 'on' week is frenetic. School lunches, hockey, homework, after-school activities—and dog shit.

"Just take a bag, buddy, and pick up the poop," I say.

#

The girls are in the kitchen when Jesse gets back. They are quiet.

"You guys aren't going to school today. I'm calling a snow day," I say.

"But it's not snowing today!" Amelia exclaims.

"Yeah, well, even better, that means we'll have the toboggan hill all to ourselves."

"Toboggan!" Emma shouts.

The moments I remember the most from my childhood are the interruptions. The days where life didn't follow the plan. Where the machinery and ritual of daily life stopped for a little while. Summer thunderstorms and winter ice storms. Snow days, when the roads were too dangerous for the school bus. There is no plan for a snow day. Nothing to do except to live it.

And that's what we're going to do today. Live a day together.

Before long, they are shrieking with laughter. Sliding down the toboggan hill and slogging back up it. I may not quite be shrieking with laughter, but my heart is warm. I feel their joy. There are no divorce lawyers on this hill and, for a little while, I find a measure of peace.

At the coffee shop after, they sit across from me. Hot chocolate with marshmallows and Danishes. Rosy cheeks and smiles. Jesse sits between Amelia and Emma, his blond curls sticking out from under his tuque. Emma is a teen now and is starting to define identity with her clothes, pink blouse and blue jeans. Amelia has chocolate on her nose; she's a free spirit.

On the way back we stop at Walmart.

"You guys can each have one thing for your room that we can use to decorate," I tell them.

The kids rush off to roam the aisles in search of that one perfect thing. I head for the home section. I'm not a decorative guy generally. My bedroom has a bed, dresser, and TV, exactly like it was set up in the showroom. No photos or trinkets. A charging station for my phone. That's it. But something catches my eye. A glass figurine. One of those mass-manufactured decorative pieces.

It might not be high art, but I'm struck by the asymmetry of a female shape melted into a man's shape. His head is bowed gently toward her forehead, his glass arms enveloping her body. Gradually the two forms melted together into a single base.

I have a few friends who are into manifestation and visualization. I don't particularly buy what they're selling. Not because I don't think it's true, but rather they are only scratching the surface of deeper spiritual concepts that have been written about for millennia. There's some wisdom to be found there, but I don't think hanging a picture of a Ferrari in your office so that one will show up in the driveway is it.

But even if it's not so simple, there is something in that figurine that speaks to me.

I enjoy solitude. I can handle being alone. But what I long for is that sense of intimacy. That place of knowing someone and being known by someone. Standing truly naked, free from all the bullshit and bluster, the fancy suit and nice watch, and being accepted and, if possible, even loved. To care and be cared for. To reach the levels of tenderness my grandparents had, the kind that takes time, takes the trials and tribulations of life and shared experience. It feels so far away from me right now, impossibly out of reach. But the glass figurine will go on my dresser as a reminder. Something I can open my eyes to in the morning and close them to at night. It's not about manifesting something in my life as much as being clear about my own truth, my deepest desire.

I place the boxed figurine gently into the cart. And then I do something stupid. I check my email. There's a message from my lawyer. Before even opening it, my heart races and my gut sinks. Fight or flight. It's the opening salvo from my ex's divorce lawyer. I scan the email to get to the numbers. Fuck.

"It's just an opening offer," my lawyer writes.

Between the throw pillows and candlesticks, I'm raging. I want to scream.

It's not the number, it's the principle. I'm okay providing for my ex-wife while she transitions to a new career. I'm not okay with the impunity with which these numbers get tossed around. Her lawyer is factoring in maximum earning potential. Basically, the years where my company, the market, and my salary were the highest. He wants to straight line that for the next decade, and take a percentage. Locked in. Guaranteed by the courts.

Easy. No problem. I'll just ask every customer to sign a ten-year contract. Paid upfront regardless of my own performance. I'll also pause the world. Make sure there are no competitors or technology disruptions that would get in the way of my ability to provided guaranteed income to my ex-wife.

I'm on autopilot. Roaming the aisles with one eye looking for the kids and the other eye completely blind, focused on the chaos inside me. I barely realize that I've found Jesse. He's tugging at my hand and I can't hear him.

"What!?" I shout.

He wants a giant blow-up karate doll. He managed to find the single most expensive toy in the store.

"We can't afford it, buddy," I tell him.

"But you said anything we wanted," he says.

I've worked my way from a paper route and part-time McDonald's job to running a small but successful global technology business. There isn't anything in this Walmart that my credit card can't handle, but I'm feeling vulnerable in all kinds of ways right now, financially especially.

"I know, Buds, but I was thinking more like twenty bucks. Not two hundred."

He nods with understanding and walks away a little slower. He doesn't look at the toys, he just walks away from me with his head down. *Shit.*

He's hurt. In the swirl of my emotional storm, I sometimes lose sight of how the kids are handling this. Their new rooms are mostly bare. They're going to need more than just one thing to make it feel like home.

"Wait, let's get the girls and do this differently," I tell him.

We find the girls and I bring them to the front of the store.

"Okay, guys, we're only going to do this once. You each get one shopping cart. Fill it up with whatever you want and meet me at the front of the store in one hour. Dad has to send a few emails," I say.

"Anything? Even the karate dummy?" Jesse asks.

"Yeah, buddy, go for it," I say.

And they go. I call my lawyer. We talk for long enough that the kids have time to fill up their carts. A three-wagon train of blue carts, almost overflowing with toys and trinkets makes its way toward the cash desks. The kids are excited. I haven't yet learned how to solve problems without creating more problems, but today, they are smiling.

CHAPTER 4 — ALLO

Fadi's been encouraging me to get out and date. If nothing else, just to get out of the house and meet people. I don't like meeting people. Between the kids, my parents, the job, and the dog, I don't have the energy. But Fadi is persistent. I relent. I give it a try.

I'm sitting in the car waiting for my date. We're meeting for the third time. First was the coffee interview. Second was a walk in the forest. Tonight, it's dinner. I'm nervous, so I arrived twenty minutes early. I play the same song over and over. Rihanna and Drake. I heard the song on the radio and liked the way it made me feel. I had to ask the kids who sang it. It has a cool rhythm. It oozes a kind of sensual chillness. And that's how I want to be tonight—chill. The song helps tone down the inner nerd.

She walks out of the building. She moves the way the music sounds, full of elegance and sensuality. She's beautiful. Totally out of my league. I'm catching her at a weak moment in her life.

Fadi helped me pick the place. Small, rustic, charming, great food and

/

ambiance. Attention to detail. I'm wearing cologne and I put cream under my eyes. I read a list of dating tips on the internet.

She sees the car and walks toward me. She moves in a way that shows she knows I'm looking. I reach over and push the car door open for her.

"Allo!" she says.

She's from the French side of town. English is her second language. French is my second language. We defaulted to French. Another reason I'm nervous. I grew up speaking French. I count in French. But I think in English. On my best day, in English I can be mildly charming and moderately funny. In French though, I'm totally ham-fisted. Each thought needs translating. I can never fully accurately express how I feel or what I think. But at least I'll be better at listening.

We drive to the restaurant, exchanging pleasantries. She's a little nervous. That surprises me. In my inventory of preconceived notions, one of them is that beautiful people are always at the height of self-confidence. She's talking and I'm listening. I like that. I like listening to her voice. She speaks softly but honestly. She's connected to herself. How she speaks is how she feels.

It's a short drive. She tells me about her day. She's an aerospace engineer but working in a job that doesn't fully engage her. She's also an artist. She loves to design and create. The house she built was featured in an architectural digest. She's looking forward to the spring; there's a type of plant that she loves that grows wild. Every spring she goes into the forest with her son and they transplant some to her place.

I'm driving and listening. She's speaking quickly, and for me, time is slowing down. I'm noticing things I don't normally. Her cadence. Her breath, almost racing. I can't tell if she's nervous or excited.

I stop in front of the restaurant.

"I'll drop you off here and meet you inside," I say.

I don't really know the right protocol. The internet didn't cover this. Should I have parked and walked in together? I didn't prepare for this. It's cold out and I don't want her to be cold.

The restaurant is everything Fadi said it would be. The vibe is similar to the song. Perfect.

She orders a glass of white wine and I order sparkling water. Tonight, I'm going to tell her everything about me that might suck. If there are any deal-breakers, let's get those out of the way early.

"You don't like wine?" she asks.

"No, I don't drink. I come from a lineage of alcoholics and problem drinkers. I stopped drinking ten years ago because I was heading to the same place they were," I say.

"Oh. Okay. I'll order something else."

"No, no. I'm not even conscious of what other people are drinking. If anything, I like it when people are drinking because they tend to get a little more relaxed. And funny."

She smiles.

"Do you miss it?"

"No. I was missing out on so much life when I did drink."

There's a pause. I look into her eyes. Internet dating tips again: Keep eye contact.

"My kids are everything to me," I blurt out. "I take care of my kids, I work and if I can, I date. I wanted you to know as much as possible about me as early as possible in case…"

"In case what?"

"I have a lot going on in my life, and I just wanted you to know who I am, I guess," I say.

"My son is everything to me. I work a job I don't like so that he can follow any dream he wants. He is with me most of the time and nothing and no one will change that," she says.

Her eyes seem to shine a little brighter when she talks about Elliott.

"There's another thing," I say.

She braces herself.

"It's possible my parents might move in with me. They aren't doing very well. My new house has a walkout basement. I want to take care of them. I don't always get along with them super well, but they're both sick in different ways and need a little help."

I wait for her reaction. I'm not just a guy on a date; I also come with a carnival tent. This circus has parents, kids, a dog, lawyers, and free popcorn.

"What happened to your parents?" she asks.

I was expecting one of two reactions: polite interest so that we could finish the meal before never seeing each other again, or the second, a firm but kind thanks but no thanks, check please. But the tone of her voice surprises me. Genuine curiosity and compassion.

"My mom has some kind of spinal issue. Her back is hunched over and she can barely look up. My dad, uh, my dad has emotional things going on. Depression, anxiety, that kind of thing. He can be a little heavy on the medication and he falls a lot. He's missing a toe from diabetes and has been on disability for the past ten years. Honestly, the situation's not great, but they're my parents and I love them."

One thing that happened in my marriage is I became unmoored from my own truth. Small compromises over time. I stopped caring for my parents the way I wanted to because it made for an easier marriage. It was a slow drift away from the man I thought I should be.

Post-marriage, becoming that man has its proper place in my life. Taking care of my parents as best I can is a core value. If it's a deal-breaker, so be it.

"I think that's nice what you are doing. I love my parents. We speak almost every day. Especially during the tough times, they call me to see how I'm doing each day. They're both on the phone at the same time. They've been married for almost forty-five years and still live in the same house."

I melt a little.

The waiter brings us each a clam chowder.

"It's delicious," she says.

It is delicious. I'm eating again. Not much but the soup is amazing. I order the lamb and she orders the fish.

"Tell me about your kids," she says.

We find easy conversation talking about the kids. I tell her about Emma starting high school.

"She was doing well for a while but now she's struggling. She met a boy. I think she fell in love, and him maybe not so much. She's quiet now and I'm worried. My boy Jesse plays hockey. Seven days a week. Fifty weeks a year. He loves it. I love watching him. Hockey culture is a little intense, but it gets me out of the house and that's a good thing. And... Amelia. She's a sparkplug. She's an unstable element in the periodic charts and I mean that in the best possible way," I say.

I ask her about Elliott and she lights up again.

"Elliot loves to build with Lego. Since he was a boy he built interesting things with Lego. He's a little older now and doesn't play as much but he's very curious. Fascinated by everything and everyone. To learn English I used to read him *The Hobbit*. He loves to read. And now soccer. He just started. In the spring it will be his second year."

"Soccer mom," I say.

"Hockey dad," she says.

"How's your fish?" I ask.

"Delicious, try some," she says.

She delicately cuts a piece and adds a few vegetables. She reaches her hand over and places the fork near my mouth. I eat it.

"Wow, that is good."

I don't like fish.

"Want to try the lamb?" I ask.

"Sure," she says, and I follow her lead, placing a little mashed potato over the lamb, cutting off a bite-size piece and raising the fork to her mouth.

There is one thing I'm a little nervous about. The internet dating site said that if you like someone and the date is going well, you should try a little bit of physical contact. Gentle, but something to bridge the friendship gap. With my kids and closest friends, I'm a hugger. But I generally don't look strangers in the eye, and touching of any kind is a conscious act for me. The article I read recommended a few techniques. Only one seems doable from where I'm sitting.

"That's a beautiful ring. Can I see it?" I ask.

"Oh, thank you, of course."

She raises her hand and I hold her fingers, pretending to look at her jewelry.

"It's beautiful." I feel a little dishonest because I don't care about the jewelry, but I feel like I've achieved an important milestone in dating life.

We leave the restaurant and I drive her to where she's parked outside her office. She leans over and kisses me on the cheek.

"Thank you for dinner. I really enjoyed myself," she says.

"My pleasure. I'll text you tomorrow, okay?" I say.

She leaves and for the first time in a while, I'm smiling. For the briefest of moments, I forget about my life.

It only lasts seconds before I feel the wave of anxiety. The lawyers. A single thought about the lawyers and my stomach starts to churn. I feel the anger building. My mind jumps around. From the lawyers to my kids, my work, my parents. My chest tightens.

I watch Nancy's car pull away and my inner nerd starts calculating loudly about statistics and probabilities. *I don't think this is going to work out.*

I've never met anyone like her before. The analyst in me tries to compartmentalize and compute. Look for patterns to compare and contrast. *No match found.* A new pattern. She is so, *feminine.* It's the label on the big mystery box in my mind where I put everything that doesn't fit inside the other boxes.

The voice is warning me. *Incompatibility.* I won't know how to be or act around her. I can't be funny or relaxed in French. I'll never be comfortable; she's so classy and I still think fart jokes are funny.

I don't have the time or energy for this. She's out of my league. She'll figure that out eventually and my heart is going to hurt again.

CHAPTER 5 — STREETLIGHT

A couple of years ago, my mom called me. "I think I need to go to the hospital. Your dad can't drive," she said.

"Okay, Mom, I'll be right there," I said.

When I arrived at their place, I opened the door and found her bent over with pain. We drove to the ER. My dad sat in the back. I watched him in the rear-view mirror. Oblivious. A mild stupor and a pleasant smile. I wasn't feeling compassion for my mom because I felt only rage toward him. Toward the doctors overprescribing and a modern medical system that steered a man so far away from dignity and grace. *Fucking take care of your wife, man.*

She got treated that night. On top of everything else, my mom had been diagnosed with breast cancer. She had been receiving chemotherapy and that resulted in some kind of mineral deficiency. After an IV drip, she felt better. We left the hospital near midnight. I drove them home and just as I turned on to the street, I caught sight of a streetlight. Tall and arched, shining down on an empty street.

Sometimes, a thing catches my attention—a symbol, a person, an object—and I'll have no idea why. My attention will linger and a kind of curiosity kicks in.

Pulling into my parent's place that night, I immediately knew why.

My mom's car was hooked up to a tow truck.

"Why are they towing my car?" she asked.

Standing outside, she watched her car being towed away with confusion.

"Where is he going?" she asked.

"Have you missed any lease payments, Mom?" I asked.

She nodded her head and started to cry. I walked to her. Put my arms around her and lowered my shoulder so her head could rest on it. My heart sank. Between the chemo and her body's reaction to the mastectomy, she had missed some shifts at Walmart. She hadn't made the payments on the car in months. I didn't know. She never told me, and I never asked.

That was the streetlight. A little bit of light in the darkness. I want to be that for her.

#

Today I'm picking her up. I'm taking her to see her new place; my basement apartment is almost ready.

I knock and she opens the apartment door. "Sorry for making you wait, love," she says with a trace of English accent. Her parents were from the north of England, and she grew up in the Midlands. Her hair is long, white, and straight now. For the longest time she had curly red hair and hated it. She lost a breast to cancer, but the chemotherapy straightened her hair and she, reasonably, considered that a fair trade. "They could have taken both my breasts for all I need them," she said after the surgery. Her eyes are fiercely blue and always look down; her back is hunched and she has to strain her neck just to glimpse the horizon.

I bring her to the house and show her the basement. It's a full apartment. Kitchen, bathroom, separate entrance, and two rooms.

"This is your new place, Mom..." I say.

I hesitate, because I'm not quite sure how to deliver the news.

"But it's just for you, Mom. Pop isn't coming."

"He doesn't want to come?"

"I don't want him to come."

I had given my dad a choice. If he wanted to move in, he had to clean up. He tried. For a month or so, he managed to kick the pills to the curb. He became lucid and there was the occasional streak of his old shining self. The quick wit and bright smile. The caring, kindness, and compassion. It's amazing, maybe even miraculous to see the transformation in a man freed from affliction. Freed from obsession and inner torment.

I had hoped for a miracle, and for a brief interval, got one. His desire to be with my mom, in a new place, lit him up. He knew the condition. Clean and sober. He almost made it. A few weeks ago, I picked him up for coffee and there he was in a stupor, dead-eyed and smiling.

There's a biblical story about Jesus casting out demons from a man into a herd of swine. The pigs then run down a hill into a lake and drown themselves. That's addiction. It's a demonic autopilot that runs a person down a hill to drown them in a lake. Demonic possession, my dad's conscience—his compassion and ability to feel and express love, feel joy, held hostage to a force he can neither understand nor control.

In her new basement apartment, my mom starts to cry.

"Are we separating?" she asks.

"Yeah, Mom. I think you need to be on your own. We can't take care of Pop when he falls over. You can't pick him up, and when I travel or I'm at work, I can't either."

"Can we at least try one last time?"

"We did try one last time, Mom. It's over."

My parents had been together through sickness and health for forty years. There was a lot more sickness than health, but there has always been a deep love between them that kept pulling them back together whenever the world pulled them apart. I don't like interfering in other people's lives. Compassion doesn't mean intervention. Suffering is an important part of a person's life because it's the catalyst for change, for growth. It's not always obvious to me when to intervene and when not, and most of the time I err on the side of not.

The last place I want to intervene is in my parents' marriage, regardless of how I may perceive it. But the practicalities of caring for my dad, mom, kids, dog—work, travelling, hockey—the math just doesn't work. So, a little bit of triage. My dad is going to have to figure this one out on his own.

#

I meet Mike at a diner. It's our favourite spot. Low key and homemade food. Club sandwiches and pea soup. Pizza and wings. A fireplace inside for the winter and fall, and a terrace outside for the spring and summer.

We are sitting on the terrace on one of the first warm days of spring.

I order the club. Mike gets the fish and chips.

"Nice to see you eating again," Mike says.

"I think club sandwiches might be what I missed most," I say.

The conversation meanders from kids to work and politics before Mike circles round to the bachelor life.

"Are you still dating that girl? What was her name again?"

"Nancy. And no. I broke up with her."

"I thought you said you'd never met anyone like her?"

"I haven't. She's amazing."

"So, you broke up with her?"

"I did the analysis. It's not going to work. I sent her a text a few weeks ago."

"Are you serious?"

"I know," I say. "Dick move."

I was shopping for groceries last month. Nancy and I had been texting. We were making plans for the weekend and somewhere between the vegetables and the dairy section I texted her to say I couldn't see her anymore. It was impulsive. A spontaneous decision. I do that sometimes. *'It's not you. It's me'* couldn't be any truer in this case.

"I'm a wreck, Mike. I spend most of my off weeks in bed. Just coming here today felt like a mountain to climb. I can't cry anymore, I can't read or watch TV, I don't feel anything. I have no desire. I just exist. She's the exact opposite of that. She's so full of life, love, beauty. She radiates it, man. Everywhere she goes. It's like the world is in black and white and she turns it into colour," I say.

"So, you broke up with her…" he repeats flatly.

"We're from different tribes, man. She's from the happy and whole people tribe and I shouldn't have even started dating in the first place. You were right. I'm not ready."

Fadi and Mike don't know each other. When Fadi was urging me to date, Mike was cautioning restraint. I liked Fadi's advice more. I rushed headlong into something I was ill prepared for. I hate it when Mike is right about something.

Mike is one of those solid people. Balanced. Generous. Caring. Disciplined. He prays but still knows how to have fun. He is of Dutch heritage, as is his wife, Anne. They aren't farmers, but sometimes I think of them that way. A couple in the community, keeping it simple, raising the kids, milking the cows, and weeding the garden.

All this to say that for Mike right now, my life is a reality TV show. I am officially off the beaten path and there's a part of him that's delighted and entertained by me rolling around in the bushes. There is a subtext to all our conversations, one where Mike is basically thinking *Brother, you don't have to flail around in the bushes like tha*t. And me thinking, *No, Mike, I got this!*

"What are you going to do?" he asks.

"I don't know, Mike. One day at a time. One foot in front of the other. I did think about becoming a monk."

Mike bursts out laughing. He roars when he laughs. I wasn't exactly joking but I'm comforted by his laughter.

"I just don't know, Mike. I don't know much of anything right now."

"How are the kids?" he asks.

"Doing well, I think, all things considered. They love the dog."

"How's that going?"

"It's a disaster. Last week I had him neutered. He had one of those giant plastic saucer guards around his head. He was so peaceful when I carried him into the house. I bonded with him then. He wasn't eating anything he wanted or shitting anywhere he wanted. The kids snuggled with him in front of the fire and for once, I left the door to my room open because I wasn't worried about him shitting on the white carpet. The vet said that it would be a couple of days before he would be back to normal."

Mike is nodding.

"That night, Mike, he hobbles into my room. Right in front of my bed. Turns to face me with his big plastic cone, looks me in the eye, and drops a big steaming mess on the carpet and then walks off. *Screw you for cutting my balls off, here you go!*"

Mike roars.

"You got a lot on your plate. Just let me know if there's anything I can do. Anything at all except dog-sit and I'm yours."

My life balance sheet: successful business and technology guy, failed husband, failed bachelor, break-even dad and son.

CHAPTER 6 — SHIPWRECKED

We're driving through the night. Fadi is beside me, sleeping. The kids are behind me, also sleeping. I've been driving for nine hours. We only have a few hours left before reaching the Atlantic.

"Fadi," I say.

"Fadi, wake up!" I whisper and nudge his arm.

"Hey. What's up? How far are we?" he asks, sleepily.

"Two hours out. Can you drive?" I ask.

"No, man. I'm beat."

"Man, you've been sleeping for five hours."

"What time is it?" he asks.

"Four-thirty a.m."

"Just one more hour," he says.

"Okay. Pass me the Red Bull."

I drink the can in one swallow. We are heading to Prince Edward Island for the weekend. Fadi had rented a cottage with the girl he had been seeing for a few weeks. They broke up and he couldn't get his money back on the rental. If there's an upside to being a divorced dad, it's being able to make spontaneous decisions. The kids came home from school yesterday. I asked them if they wanted to take a road trip across the country for the weekend. They said yes. I unpacked their lunch pails, grabbed toothbrushes and whatever clothes we thought we might need, and jumped in the car. We picked up Fadi and started driving.

I like driving at night with the kids because they sleep. No fighting in the back seat. They sleep, they dream. My hope is to get to the Atlantic at sunrise so they can fall asleep in the city and wake up by the ocean.

I've never been to Prince Edward Island, but I've heard only good things. About the island and people. Winding roads, hillsides, lobster. Seals, fishing, clam digging along a red sandy beach that stretches as far as the eye can see.

Driving eastbound, I see the signs of dawn. The first sign of colour on the horizon, deep purple and red. I'm racing to the ocean before they wake up.

"Fadi… Fadi…" I say quietly.

He wakes up.

"You have to drive. We only have an hour and I'm not going to make it," I say.

I'm struggling to stay awake.

I pull the car over and we switch positions.

"You mind if I put the radio on? It'll help me drive," he says.

"Sure, man, just don't wake the kids up."

"You okay to talk for a bit or you want to sleep?"

"I'm starting to drool, man. I just need an hour and some coffee."

Fadi nods. He raises the volume slightly and I fall asleep to techno music and the rhythm of the tires on the pavement.

#

BEEEEEEEEEPPPPPPPPPP

"What the hell is that?" I shout.

I'm suddenly fully awake. It's daylight. The car is stopped at a green traffic light in the middle of a small town. I look to my left and Fadi is fast asleep at the wheel. Head tilted over.

"FADI!" I shout.

He wakes. His head shoots up, looks around, and sees the green light.

BEEEEEEEEEEPPPPPPPPPP

The car behind us honks again. Without even looking up Fadi floors the gas and we shoot through the light.

"Pull over at the next stop, man!" I say.

"I'm so sorry!" he says.

We're both a little bewildered. But the kids are in the back laughing. *Jesus, Fadi.* I shake my head a little.

"Is that the ocean?" Amelia asks.

Before us is blue ocean and whitecaps. The Atlantic. We made it. They woke up by the ocean.

We arrive at the cottage. The kids rush outside to explore. Fadi is unpacking and I head straight for the bed.

"I'm just going to try and get an hour, okay?" I say to him.

"For sure, man, I'll keep an eye on them. Don't worry," he says, looking me right in the eyes reassuringly.

#

I wake up to silence. Sunlight filtering through the wood-paned window. It feels like midday. I walk outside looking for the kids. The cottage sits alone on a few acres of empty fields. At the edge of the property is a small cliff and I walk toward it. I hear laughter.

Reaching the edge, I can see the ocean, the tide swept out to the horizon. Red-brown wet sand and a cloudless sky. I see outlines in the distance. Fadi, Emma, Jesse, and Amelia. They are digging for clams. Every time one of the kids finds a clam, laughter. I sit on the edge of the cliff and soak the moment in.

Amelia sees me and waves.

"Dad! Dad!" she shouts.

I walk down the steps and onto the long stretch of beach.

"Look at all the clams!" she says.

She lifts a bucket filled to the brim with clams. Then Jesse and Emma do the same in turn, delighted with their full buckets.

"I found the biggest one!" Jesse says.

He's competitive. So is Amelia. Emma less so; she's the eldest, the big sister, the caregiver and maybe at times, something of a surrogate mom, at least to Jesse. There's always been a weird tension between Emma and Amelia. Something I never really understood until Mike told me to google sibling rivalry. I've always had an easier time with Jesse. My daughters can fluctuate between being cruel, nurturing, moody, mysterious, gentle, and loving. As a toddler, Jesse liked to see how far he could stretch his penis and ran everywhere as fast as he could.

They seem to love digging for clams on the beach together. And they love Fadi. They are so happy and carefree around him. Fadi has a gift with the kids. He can play and engage with them in a way that I'm envious of. I can never seem to quite reach a place of not being serious. I can't dance. I watch people on TV dancing sometimes in utter fascination. Not so much for the way they move but why they are moving like that in the first place.

Clam digging might be fun but it's pointless. We're not going to eat them and I'm not planning on participating until Amelia pulls my hand.

"Come on, Dad!" she says.

We walk along the beach together, her little hand pulling mine until we find a spot.

"Here," she says. And we dig together.

"Found one!" I say.

She seems to delight more in me finding a clam than if she had found one herself. She is beaming.

#

After dinner, it's not long before the kids are all asleep. I can only sing one part of one song. It's the same song my dad used to sing to me. "You Are My Sunshine." Every night and some mornings my dad would rub my hair and sing me the only verse he knew. One by one, I do the same for each child. I rub their hair and sing the verse. Off-key but softly enough that it doesn't matter.

In the living room, Fadi lies on the couch and I sit on a velvet armchair.

"Your kids are amazing, man, you must be so proud," he says.

"I am. I'm grateful," I say flatly.

"What's wrong?"

"Today was good, man. I'm just... On Sunday they're going to go back to their mom's. And then it's a shitty week alone. Me and the dog and my mom downstairs."

"How is your mom?"

"She's okay, she's resilient. We're doing our best with the situation," I say.

"Situation?"

"The part where I'm almost forty years old and I live with my mom."

"She lives with you, man, there's a difference."

"Sure. I'll put that as an asterisk the next time I put up a dating profile."

"Are you going to start dating again?"

"Hell no."

"Ever?"

"My week with the kids is bliss. I'm busy. I take care of them. The small wounds that need healing, I tend to. I can make them laugh. Show them the world. They adore my mom. She's teaching them how to bake. We watch movies. I'm happy. The off week is the opposite of that, but I work. I catch up on all the shit I didn't do while I had the kids. I wouldn't have designed my life this way, but it is what it is and it's fine."

"How's the legal stuff going?"

"Still a mess. We've made a few offers that keep getting rejected. The last one paid better than what the cash for life lottery pays. Literally. The ex's lawyer is grinding the bill cycle. I know her well enough to know that at some point, she's going to start getting irritated by the monthly bills and then we'll settle on something short of insane."

"Sounds like you need to get away."

"Get away?"

"A vacation," he says.

"We are on vacation."

"No, I mean just you."

"Like *Stella Got her Groove Back*?" I ask.

"Maybe, but just get away, go somewhere. You have a week without the kids, and your mom can handle Theo. Let's go to Maui!"

"Hawaii?" I say.

"I was there last year after my divorce. It's healing, man, it truly is. There's something mystical about the place. I'm telling you it will change your life," he says.

I try but can't think of a good reason not to go. Other than a worry that my ex-wife and her lawyer will hear about the trip and use it as evidence of a hidden treasure trove.

There's a part of me that wants to get as far away from here as possible. To run away. The point on the globe that is opposite my city is probably somewhere in Southeast Asia. Cambodia maybe. That's where I want to go; as far away as I can get from my home. But I need to get there and back in seven days, maybe ten if I can work something out with the ex.

CHAPTER 7 — GREEN SEA TURTLES

Fadi is excited. "Finally. One last flight to go. Can't wait for you to see Maui!" he says.

We are sitting in the departure lounge at LAX.

It's been a busy week. We've travelled all over the west coast of the US for work. Two meetings a day. Fadi does sales and relationships, I do technology. It's a good combo.

"I'm looking forward to it. No work. No lawyers. No dates. Just chilling," I say.

"What do you want to do first? There's this amazing beach. The volcano—"

"Let's just chill, man. No plans. Ten days with no plans. Just that is enough for me."

"Are you still going to want to do stuff?"

"C'mon, yeah of course, I just don't want to schedule it ahead of time. Let's just decide on the day."

Fadi has been active in the dating scene and this is the longest spell he's been single now—a couple of weeks. He's agitated. Nervy. He needs to move. His marriage lasted a couple of years. He didn't see the end coming. He's good natured about it now but it was rough.

He was travelling when he found out. He called me from an airport. He rather stoically shared the facts before completely breaking down. He was in line for boarding and howling like a wounded animal.

He has bounced around semi-serious relationships since, from two weeks to a couple of months. Usually with no more than a week's gap between.

"Did you ever hear back from that lady you brought to the Christmas party?" I ask.

"Ugh," he sighs and we both laugh.

Fresh from the divorce, Fadi fell in love on the first date. After two weeks, confident enough in the bonds of their relationship, he moved all his stuff into her father's garage. The father, a Greek, was incredibly proud his daughter had finally met a good, hardworking man. At three weeks, he brought her to the office Christmas party. By Christmas they had split up.

"That damn snowstorm," he says, laughing.

In January, he rented a large truck to go pick up his stuff at his almost father-in-law's, a man he had known only a few weeks. There was a snowstorm. Visibility was restricted. Fadi backed up into a ditch. The truck was at a 30-degree angle, stuck in deep snow, a hundred feet from the man's house. Sheepishly, he made his way up the driveway and asked the man for help. The Greek had to call a friend. The friend brought a tractor. Took the better part of the day before they pulled the truck out of the ditch and Fadi could get his stuff out of the man's garage.

That's Fadi. The buccaneer. Living from moment to moment. "No dates on this trip, okay, man? I just want to hang out with you, chill, and experience the island," I say.

"Of course, man, that's not where my head was at either. I'm looking forward to showing you around," he says.

#

We are driving a bright red Jeep with the top open along the winding road to Hanna. Lush forests, spectacular ocean views, incredibly rich smells. The weather is sunny and warm with the gentlest of breezes. For most people, this is probably a good start to a day, but I'm grumpy. I'm quiet and sullen.

"You okay?" Fadi asks.

"I'm fine. When does this road end, it's been like an hour?" I ask tersely.

"I think another hour. We don't have to come back the same way, though. We can try and go around the island."

I feel shitty for putting this on Fadi. We've been on the island for two days. Yesterday we visited the volcano at the crack of dawn. We watched the sunrise above the clouds. When the clouds cleared, we looked into the otherworldly crater. On the outside, I oohed and aahed like all the other tourists, but on the inside, all I kept thinking was how cold it was.

On the road to Hanna, in the heart of paradise, all I can think about is how long the road is... and winding. Always fucking winding. Every hundred feet or so, winding.

"I'm hungry," I say.

I sound like a child.

"There's a roadside taco truck not too far away," he says.

We finally pull into some kind of hippie compound, full of old trailers in bright colours. A surfboard stands to one side, "Aloha" painted down its length. Beside it, a wooden sign: *The Best Coconut Candy, 6.00 a bag.* We sit down on a bench with more fish tacos than we can possibly eat, but I'm going to try. Halfway through the second, my mood lightens.

"Do you think you're enlightened?" Fadi asks.

I swallow and think for a moment.

"Who's asking the question?" I ask.

"What do you mean?"

"Well, you're asking if I'm enlightened. Baked into the question is a point of view that there's a you and there's a me. Some schools of Buddhism focus a lot on this, this notion of separation and that it's actually an illusion. It gets pretty hard to talk about using words, but I'd say there is a state I can reach where I don't sense that separateness, that I feel connected. That you and I having a conversation feels more like two waves moving through an ocean. It's a sense, a feeling, more than a belief," I say.

"So you're enlightened?"

"I can probably hang out with some monks and have a good time."

"So then why are you so grumpy all the time?"

Ouch.

"We are literally in paradise and you've been walking around kicking your lunch pail," he says.

"I know. I'm sorry," I say. "This thing inside me... this... feeling. It's like hatred. I'm so fucking angry. I don't know what to do.

Being one with a taco isn't making it go away. Being present to it, understanding it, isn't helping either. I've been trying the exercises in that blue book on miracles, and sometimes there, I can get a little bit of distance. A little bit of space between me and the hatred, but it lasts for seconds. Then it's like this thing has its own gravity and it pulls me right back in."

"Is that what you were doing this morning?"

"Yeah. The chapter was on anguish, that the source of all my pain is that I'm holding on to something that is of no value. That I need to let that go and hold on to something that does have value. That there is only one thing that does have value."

"What's that?"

"My capacity for love."

"Jesus said that?"

"Maybe. It doesn't matter. It resonated with me and that matters. But I can't seem to put it into practice, clearly, and that matters," I say.

We grab a few bags of coconut candy and drive. Between the tacos, the candy, and the conversation with Fadi, I feel a little happier. I think I'm starting to enjoy the drive. The colour palette of life's exuberance—deep greens and blues, the bright white in the churn and chop of the sea on the rocks. We arrive at the hideaway beach.

We park and walk down a set of stairs along a cliffside.

The beach sand is almost black. Volcanic. And in this small bay, the waves are massive. The height of two men standing on top of one another.

"I brought us some boogie boards. Follow me and do what I do," Fadi instructs.

Then he teaches me how to boogie board. How to feel the incredible power of these waves without a spinal injury. By the third wave, I find myself near the crest, suspended almost in midair and free. I feel the power of the ocean in this wave before I roll, twist, and turn onto the sand below.

"Amazing!" I shout.

"Yeah!" he shouts back.

For an hour or maybe more, I'm just a boy. A boy and a boogie board, playing in the waves and sand.

Lying on our beach towels and soaking in paradise. Sharing it with only a small handful of souls.

"Thank you," I say.

#

We keep driving around the island. This time, I drive the narrow cliffside roads around the back of the volcano. We stop to put the roof on the Jeep as we drive through microclimates, and enjoy the rain knowing that in only a few minutes we will be back in the sunshine.

My heart starts to open with gratitude and appreciation for the man sitting in the passenger seat. The man who has been with me in my darkest of hours. A man who is as patient as he is kind.

"You think you'll have kids one day?" I ask him.

"I don't know. Sometimes I think I'm too selfish. I like my life the way it is. But then I see you, I see my friends with their kids, and a part of me wants that also. I just don't think I'm ready."

"I don't think you ever get ready. I'm fourteen years in and there are still days I know I'm not ready for. I think you'd be an amazing dad, Fadi."

"Really?"

"Yeah, of course, man. You know how to be present, you can truly *be* with someone. The kids feel that. They know when you are with them. Emma looks at me sometimes and waves. She tries to get my attention because she knows I'm not with her. I'm somewhere far away, deep inside my mind. Trying to solve problems, anticipating the future, replaying the past."

"I do that too."

"So does everyone. But that presence you have around the kids, your ability to just hang and live a moment with them. That's a skill and you're good at it. I devote myself to ritual and practice, and only on rare occasions am I able to string a few consecutive minutes of presence together. I work hard just to get to the place you are at naturally," I say.

"I guess we'll see. I have to meet the right woman first and I know for sure I'm not ready for that."

We laugh. We drive. He tells me more dating stories and we laugh some more.

"I want to show you the turtles," he says.

We drive north toward Paia and stop at a small parking lot on the slope of a hill. We walk from the car down the hillside toward a beach.

"There," Fadi says, pointing.

"The rocks?" I ask.

"No, man, those are turtles."

We walk closer.

"Holy shit, there's like a hundred of them!" I exclaim in wonder.

A hundred sea turtles on the beach. Shells and a few heads poking out in the evening sunshine. *Just chillin'.* One of the turtles is paddling her flippers, inching her way up the beach to be closer to the pack.

There's a line in the sand. Someone has dragged their heel through the dirt. It was an invisible barrier of goodwill. *Don't touch the turtles, let them chill.* And nobody did. We obeyed the protocol of the line in the sand and just watched these magnificent creatures.

I like that. The line in the sand. Some hipster just figured out a way of protecting the turtles from tourists. I make a mental note about systems, minds, people, and organizations. *An invisible barrier of goodwill.*

#

Fadi is still asleep. I drink my coffee on the porch and stare out at the trees. We are staying in a cabin near the main house in the middle of an orchard. The man that rented us the place bought the land a decade ago. He and his wife planted trees while their daughter was still young. Today she is at university. Her tuition is literally paid for by the fruits of her mom and dad's labour: dragon fruit, guava, and lychee. Harvested, collected, and sold at the local market.

The property is secluded. There's dew on the grass. My phone blinks with an incoming text message.

Are you in Hawaii?
It's a message from my ex. I was dreading her finding out and have been deliberately vague about my trip. *Technically it was a business trip.* I haven't missed any monthly support payments, but the optics of a Hawaii trip during a legal negotiation aren't great.

Yes, I text back.

Is it as beautiful as they say?
More.
Good for you. Enjoy it. The kids are doing well.

I wasn't expecting that. After almost a year of acrimony and insanity, a nonthreatening message. I'm dubious. The scars run deep. But the conversation continues and before long, we are both in tears. It's not reconciliation; it's something better. She sends me photos of the kids while I've been away. I send her photos from the past few months, from Prince Edward Island, from the snow day.

They're amazing, she says.

Somehow, we did okay there, eh? I say.

We did. I'm crying, I text her.

So am I, she replies.

For a moment, we find each other. Not as combatants in a legal dispute, not as boyfriend and girlfriend or husband and wife, but as human beings. And the feeling of humanity is intense. Free from all the social expectations, I suddenly feel something pure inside me. I see her in a different light: a fellow traveller. It's a new feeling. The kind of thing I might feel for a helpful stranger on a long plane journey. A generic sense of goodwill and shared destiny without any attachment.

"You okay?" Fadi asks.

I didn't hear him wake up but he's standing beside me.

"Yeah... yeah I am."

"You're crying," he says.

"I'm happy."

"What happened?" he asks.

"I think I actually feel forgiveness... the hatred... it's gone... I feel... free."

My heart is working again. I feel it beating strong happy beats.

I had been reading the blue book and doing the exercises daily. Trying to let go. To forgive. To find a kind of peace and innocence within my being so that I could one day love again, without bitterness and insecurity. Here in Maui, between the turtles and the volcano, my dear friend Fadi and a few gentle words from my ex-wife, I feel whole, and with a kind of gratitude that I haven't felt in a long time.

#

Fadi and I are on the red-eye back home. He's fast asleep beside me. I can't sleep. I'm bouncing. I haven't felt this much energy in years because I can't wait for my phone to work again. A thought popped into my head just after we boarded. An impulse. A feeling.

I'm so happy, I need to share this with Nancy.

We land. Taxi to the terminal and finally, the bars on my signal indicator go to full. I send Nancy a message. It's a picture of the turtles.

Just getting back from Maui. It's incredible. You need to see that place!

"What are you so happy about?" Fadi asks me.

"I just sent Nancy a note about the trip."

"When was the last time you talked to her?"

"Few months ago."

"How'd that go?"

"Not great? It's when we broke up," I say.

"And you're texting her now, out of nowhere? You don't think that's a little weird?"

He's right. The truth is I wasn't thinking at all. My heart is singing so loud that my inner analyst sits in the corner with his earplugs, sulking.

My phone flashes with an incoming text.

So beautiful. Good for you, Nancy says.

I show Fadi the text.

"What do I say now?" I ask.

"Well what do you want?" he asks.

"I want to marry her."

"Okay. Don't say that. You haven't seen or spoken to her in months. You don't know her situation or how she feels about you. Say nothing. Just take it slow."

"Okay," I say.

I look down at my phone and start typing.

"What are you doing?"

"Texting Nancy."

"Texting what?"

"That I want to take it slow."

"I don't understand how you can be so wise about life yet such a complete moron about relationships. Just say nothing, man," he insists. "First, you've only just now thought of this. Second, she hasn't heard from you in months. Slow down. Just see how you feel in a few days. Then see how she feels. She probably has quite a few people trying to woo her right now if she isn't already in a relationship. Man, just slow down. And this is coming from the guy who almost got married three times this year."

"Okay," I say and delete the text in progress, completely betraying my heart.

What I wanted to say:

"Nancy, I want to take you to Maui. I want to show you the turtles. I want to take you around the world and see it through your eyes. I want to listen to your sweet voice tell me your dreams and hopes because you are the most incredible person I have ever met. Everything and everyone you touch becomes more beautiful. You are dignity, grace, elegance, and adventure. You are a wellspring of love for this world and I want to marry you. Coffee?"

What I actually say:

Yeah, it's a very nice place.
Mediocrity. And she doesn't text anything back.

CHAPTER 8 — CHRISTMAS

It's been almost two months since I got back from Maui. I've reached out to Nancy a few times and been gently rebuffed each time. Normally, I'd be a little down, but I've just landed in Dubai and there is a big Christmas tree in the airport.

This city lights me up inside. Walking through Dubai Airport customs hall, bobbing along a river of humanity. I feel energized every time I come through this airport. I love people-watching here. Thousands of people from all over the world streaming through the immigration gates; African dashikis in primary colours; Arabians in blazing white kanduras and raven black abayas; Europeans in jeans; and Indians and Asians in business suits. The morning rush of inbound traffic, we flow together into the customs hall.

There's a sign with a wheelchair symbol that reads 'people of determination.' If I could summarize this place in a sentence, that would be it. A nation of determination.

I've been coming here for work since 2008. The very first customer for our start-up technology company was in the UAE. Lots of preconceived notions about the region were shattered for me. What I thought would be a culture of authority and religious extremism turned out to be tolerant and pragmatic; the largest bookstore in the country has a religious section that stocks the Qur'an, the Bible, Buddhist teachings, Hindu and Hebrew scriptures, wisdom from the Dao, and writings from the Four Horseman—the modern atheists.

I've dealt with more women in power and authority in this region than I have back home. Almost everyone is here to work, to pursue a dream and make their life a little bit better. The starting point for the journey is different for all of us, but almost everyone here shares the same aspiration: upward and onward.

The city itself, the architecture, the ambition, the buzz—inspiring and uplifting. The beauty of the human endeavor and a world in motion. It all happens so fast here, at such an incredible scale that you can witness evolution almost in real-time. When I share this with my friends back home, they talk about modern slavery, labour and sex trade, the oppression of women and censorship. And we argue. I point out some of our own culture's shortcomings along similar lines. Our own less than exemplary history, and in some cases, present. But it remains an argument and I've had enough of that for one life.

I'm fascinated by a modern nation of city-states that still embrace religion. There are over two hundred different nationalities living here, and probably only a fraction are Islamic. But the call to prayer,

Ramadan, temperance, creates an undeniable vibe. A mix of chill, unity, devotion, creativity, and industry.

I jump in a taxi and head toward the Burj Khalifa: the tallest building in the world. At the base of the Burj is a shopping centre, the nicest I've ever seen in terms of architecture—the flow, the vibrant colours and style. The dance between form and function creates an orchestra of a design. Beauty, cohesion, and harmony—the mall is a symphony.

I sit in a café watching the fountains outside. I take a picture of the skyscraper and send it to Nancy.

Incredible, she texts back.

She had called me the other day. She asked me not to send her any more flowers. We spoke for almost an hour. I asked if it was okay to keep in touch. She said yes. Her responses are usually short but not quite curt.

The mall has a giant Christmas tree, tastefully decorated. The shops play the familiar jingles. I'm hoping for a Christmas miracle. Unrequited love might be better than living without desire, but it's not easy. The feelings of hopelessness and despair. The fool's errand. *Don't give up*, I keep telling myself.

I walk the floors looking for a gift for Nancy and her son. Something gentle but thoughtful. Friendly but with a hint of romance. I settle on a coffee table book of Dubai architecture for Nancy; she loves architecture and travel and I'd love to bring her here one day. For Elliott, a Lego set of the Burj Khalifa. I spend the rest of the morning shopping for my kids.

#

I call Mike from the hotel to catch up.

"You still chasing Nancy?" Mike asks.

"Yeah. She hasn't asked for a restraining order yet."

"You can't take no for an answer," he chides.

"Well, she didn't exactly say no."

"She told you she was with someone."

"Ya, well, fuck that guy!"

"Is this about you winning or is this really about Nancy?"

"I can't get her out of my head, Mike. More importantly, I can't get her out of my heart. I tried. I thought about dating again, but it's not my truth. I have to live out what's in my heart."

"What about what's in her heart?"

"That's not up to me. It's her truth and I don't know what that is, but

I'm trying to live as honestly as possible, to act on what my heart says and not what I think the world wants. I'm in love with her, Mike."

"You barely know her. She's not in love with you. She's dating someone else. You've sent flowers and Christ knows what else. I'm worried about you," he says.

"Don't be. I'm in a good place."

"What does all your spiritual stuff say about this?"

"It says to pursue the girl you're in love across the galaxy and to never give up."

"Really?"

"No. No, it doesn't. The Christian book is about universal and cosmic love. The Buddhist teachings I've come across tend to bracket desire as a problem that needs to be solved. The Hindus, though, seem to explore it a little more."

"You're picking and choosing from different religions so you can chase a woman?"

"I'm not picking or choosing anything. It's all just wisdom to me. Some of it resonates, some of it doesn't. They're just words on a page. Deep truths, maybe, in some cases, but if you think the complete truth about this universe or God can fit inside a few pages, you're missing the point. Me. I'm truth. You. You're truth. And my truth right now is that I want to pursue Nancy."

"Just don't get arrested."

"It's a fine line."

I don't want to cross into stalker territory. I'm aiming for gentle but persistent. I asked Nancy out for coffee. I sent flowers, some chocolates. There's a new service in town that delivers fresh cupcakes. I did that too. More flowers. Each time, she's been graceful, says thanks. Declined my offer for coffee, out of respect to the person she is with. But the feeling I get in our interactions is *keep trying*.

I don't think equanimity is the absence of desire but rather being chill with it. It's accepting not just the world as it is, but my own self, my feelings and deepest desires. The moon is barren and free from desire of any kind. This planet is full of desire. Full and longing. Entanglement. Suffering. Competition and cooperation. Victories and defeats. Life. I'm from Earth, not Moon.

"How's the legal stuff going?" Mike asks.

"It's all over. My lawyer told me straight up when we started the process: 'When you marry a woman, and I say specifically if you are the man and you marry a woman, because that's still generally how the judges view the world—when you marry a woman, you damage her. The amount of damage you cause her is dictated by the amount of time you are together and how many kids you have together. The emotional specifics of each case don't matter. What matters is your ability to make her whole on the damage.'"

"It is what it is, marriage in the twenty-first century... accrual of damages," I explain. "Nobody is going to shed a tear for a wealthy white guy. I wouldn't put my signature on anything I couldn't live with. They wouldn't put me in jail because then the lawyers won't get paid. It worked out."

"Good. Time to move on with your life."

#

It's a short trip. A few presentations and meetings before travelling back home. I sit on a bench near my hotel, soaking in the city before my flight out tonight. My mind changes when I'm here. I feel a little more expansive, optimistic, and connected with myself.

I wrestle with the hope and pragmatism of reconnecting with Nancy. Mike is right. I've been trying for a few months. Fadi is a little more encouraging: *Follow your heart, swing for the fences, never quit!* The math though. The analyst in me says Mike is right. But my heart, my heart says to chase her across the universe.

Christmas is around the corner. Mistletoe and miracles.

#

It's Christmas Day. I'm driving the snowy winter roads to pick up the kids. Fadi and I rented a cottage for the holidays. We're doing the bachelor version of Christmas with the kids, which is basically a food bonanza, free-for-all for three straight days. Chocolate for breakfast? Sure. Chips for lunch? Go for it. Xbox all night? Sleep when you want, guys.

I can't give the kids any kind of tradition that I grew up with anymore. The one with midnight mass and family gatherings. Turkey dinner and a blessing. So, this year, at least, we're trying something different.

Christmas Eve was always more special to me than the day that followed. Growing up, there was something special about the night, dressing up as a family. My dad putting on his suit. My mom laying out the clothes we had to wear. Driving to my grandparents. Eating as a large extended family. Christmas carols and mass. Watching the adults kneel in front of my grandfather while he prayed with gratitude for the year gone by and blessed each member for the year ahead. He could never get through more than a few words without choking up, overwhelmed with gratitude.

Last night I spent mopping the floor of a small health clinic. A friend of mine is a cleaner who works the night shift. I was feeling lonely, verging on self-pity, until I remembered that my buddy spends every Christmas Eve by himself, cleaning. He doesn't have a family to miss.

I met him at the clinic and gave him a hand. After only a few minutes, he asked me to stop mopping because I was doing a terrible job. He let me play with the strap-on vacuum instead. Okay, so maybe I slowed him down more than I helped, but there was a little bit of fraternity and fellowship on an otherwise cold night.

It wasn't a selfless act. I needed the company, but in a secret compartment in the recesses of my mind, I sometimes wonder if there isn't a benevolent dictator behind the scenes. So somehow, if I do something noble, I'll get rewarded. That maybe, just maybe, if I help a friend mop a floor on Christmas Eve, Nancy will call me on Christmas Day.

It's a childish notion and Nancy didn't call.

I pull into the driveway at my old house and the kids rush out. They are excited.

"What did you get us?" Jesse asks.

"We'll see, buddy," I say.

The kids have never been to midnight mass. Emma was baptized but Amelia and Jesse weren't. It wasn't so much a philosophical decision rather the fact that a religious ceremony just seemed like one more thing to do on a great big list of things to do, jettisoned when things got busy.

They don't know much about Buddha, Jesus, or any religious figure other than what they might have picked up on TV or the occasional mention at school. Part of me wanted to teach them, build up tradition and some kind of value system, but another part of me didn't want to steer them toward something I wasn't fully confident in. At some level, bad religion is worse than no religion. It's been an inconclusive argument I've had with myself since Emma was baptized. So I try to split the difference and share the best parts, the beautiful things I've discovered in religion. My own experience and interpretation.

"I'm going to tell you guys a story. It's a long car ride. We have time," I say.

I tell them a story of a man who was kind to strangers. A man who ignited a spark of love in people that reverberated through millennia. I tell them about innocence, kindness, generosity of spirit, and fraternal and eternal love. It's a story that moved me as a child, and in retelling it again to the kids, I have to hold back tears. The kids aren't quite as impressed.

"Pops. Is it over?" Jesse asks.

"Yeah, buddy, it's over," I say.

"Can we listen to some music?" Emma asks.

"Yes, we can listen to some music. Christmas music though, okay?" I say.

\#

The kids don't make it much past the early evening before they are asleep. Fadi and I pick up the shreds of wrapping paper, the empty boxes of chocolate and chip bags, the half glasses of eggnog and soda cans. Only two wrapped gifts are left by the fireplace. For Nancy and Elliott. The coffee table book and the Lego set. I was hoping for a Christmas miracle. To deliver them in person. For Nancy to open her gift and for us to live happily ever after.

"Did she call?" Fadi asks.

"No."

"You okay?"

"Yeah. Today was a good day, man. The kids were so happy. They had fun. Thanks for being with us. I couldn't have done this without you."

"Hard to see you down again at Christmas."

"I know, man, I'm sorry. I have to let go and that's never been easy for me to do," I say.

"Plenty of fish in the sea?"

"Nah, I'm not going through this again. After his divorce, my maternal grandad was a single guy. He was happy. He took care of his grandkids, lived a good life. You don't have to be with someone to be happy."

"Dude, you're not even forty yet."

"Yeah, but I've been around. My cup is full. I'll be fine. I don't need to date."

"Well, it's not like I have all the answers," he says, laughing.

"Thank you for exposing that world of dating apps. Not for me," I say.

I'm not cynical. Just resigned. Making my way toward being grateful for the experience. Trying to look forward to what else I can be or do in this life outside of being in a relationship. I'm a better dad, son, and friend than I was a year ago. I'm productive at work again. My heart is a little sore but not so much that I can't laugh.

"I'm going to send her one last note," I say.

"Ah, stop, it's getting weird."

"I know. Just one last one. Not today. I'll wait until New Year's Eve. I'm waiting for something in the mail."

"What's that?"

"Ah it's a little weird, man, I kind of want to keep this one to myself," I say.

"Really, after everything we've been through, you're worried about what I might think?"

"It's a nose."

"What?"

"It's a prosthetic nose... like the ones the actors use."

"You're sending her a prosthetic nose? What is wrong with you?"

"No, no, I'm going to glue the nose on and take a selfie. I'm going to send a note on New Year's Eve. Something from my heart. Her favourite book is *Cyrano de Bergerac*. He had a big nose and spoke from his heart."

"I'm cringing. Seriously, don't do it, man! That is too weird."

"Yeah, but I never do anything weird. I've been keeping it between the lines my whole life and look where it's got me. I've accepted that it's not going to work out and I won't bug her after New Year, but I just wanted to go down swinging."

\#

The kids are spending New Year's at their mom's. I'm spending it in bed, binge-watching a new series on Netflix. Only a few episodes left and an hour to go before midnight. I head to the washroom to try on the nose.

I put the nose on with the skin glue the instructions recommend. *Fadi was right.* I look ridiculous. I take a few selfies with different light until I manage to get one with just the right shade.

I draft a note. I edit. Re-edit. Strip out words, add others until it's just right.

I switch from Netflix to regular TV and watch the Times Square countdown. I'm waiting for midnight. I wait with a kind of peaceful resignation. My note to Nancy is sincere. Our paths crossed. She inspired something in me and I'm grateful. It wasn't the ending I had hoped for, but I'm a better man for having known her.

The ball is coming down. The crowd is cheering. "Auld Lang Syne" starts ringing out. My heart is warmed by seeing the shared human experience, the goodwill and hope. It's a bittersweet moment.

I hit send and shut my phone off. I don't want to torture myself waiting and hoping for a response.

Dearest Nancy – I wanted to wish you the happiest of New Years, and wherever your heart may lead you in this new year, my wish for you in 2014 is this: that your gentle soul finds peace and warmth, that your year is full of tender moments, of joy, adventure, and wonder with Elliott and all those that you hold dear. That your heart soars. That you wake up every day feeling cherished, loved, and cared for and mostly that you keep being the shining light of a woman to everybody that you meet, inspiring others with your kindness, your beauty, your strength, and your grace. And a ridiculous picture of me with the elongated nose. No explanation or qualifier. Just a vain hope.

CHAPTER 9 — FORTIETH

"Surprise!"

It's summertime. I open a cedar gate to the patio on top of a boathouse, and there's a crowd. The kids are beside me. There are decorations around the old cedar structure overlooking the lake and hill of a national park. Everyone in the crowd is dressed in a Hawaiian theme; floral dresses, long shirts, brightly coloured lei garlands.

"Happy birthday, Dad!" Amelia says.

I am surprised. It's my fortieth birthday and my family is here.

"Happy birthday, man!" Fadi says and hugs me.

"Pop!" I say when I see my dad. He looks good. Kind of sober. I'm glad he came; he missed the memo about the Hawaiian theme and he's wearing socks and sandals, but he's here. He hugs me and wishes me a happy birthday.

I'm overwhelmed. I look around at the faces of the people I love. My eyes scan the crowd and then I see her. Colourful lei in her hair and a long white dress. Blue-green eyes and auburn hair glowing in the afternoon sun.

She walks slowly toward me, looks me in the eyes, and kisses me on the lips.

"Happy birthday," she says.

"Baby, I can't believe you did this. I don't know what to say."
"Say nothing. Enjoy your birthday," Nancy says.

The last six months have been a whirlwind.

We met again in January. She agreed to meet me for coffee and a skate along the frozen canal. She had left the other guy over Christmas and relented on the coffee after the new year. She opened the door to me, just a crack. Face to face again over coffee, Nancy was reserved. A little tentative. We spoke. I apologized for the way I ended our brief relationship. She listened, but more she watched. She looked in my eyes. *Can I trust you?*

It was a mild day for January. A windless winter day that a little bit of skating was all you needed to stay warm. And we did. Every winter, the canal that bisects the city freezes and becomes one of the longest skating rinks in the world. We skated and we talked some more. She asked about the kids, my parents, business and life.

I asked about Elliott, her work and her art, her designs. We lost track of time. It started to get dark.

Mid-sentence, Nancy tripped. She stumbled for a bit, then fell forward onto the ice. I couldn't move quickly enough to grab her arm, so I just threw myself on the ice beside her. She looked at me strangely.

"Why are you on the ice?" she asked.

"I don't know," I said.

She looked in my eyes again and she started laughing. She realized something at that moment, before I did. I was connected to her. I didn't want to save her because she didn't need saving. I just wanted to be by her side. *Maybe I can trust you.*

After the skating, we walked together to her car. She put her skates in the trunk, turned to me, and just said, "Thank you for the coffee." I tried to kiss her, but she turned her face slightly and gave me her cheek. She smiled. "This was nice. Maybe in a few weeks we can see each other again." I'm not a 'maybe in a few weeks' kind of a guy. But she is that kind of woman. We split the difference and went for dinner and a movie the following week.

We spoke over dinner.

"I like being with you, but I'd like to take it slow," she said.

"Sure. I understand. Is Elliott with you next week?" I asked.

"No, he's with his dad."

"Perfect," I say.

"Why?"

"I bought us tickets to the Dominican Republic. We fly out on Monday."

She laughed. "That's not slow! I don't know if I can get the time off."

"But you're considering it!" I said.

"Yes."

"I didn't actually get the tickets, but I checked all the details. If you can get the time off, let's just go!"

She likes to be in control. So do I. But I can't control my heart anymore. I don't want to even try. We spent Valentine's Day in the Dominican Republic.

By March, we introduced the kids to each other. We went bowling. Girls versus boys. The girls won. In April, it was the parents and extended family. Sugar bush and maple syrup. Then it was roller coasters and the aquarium.

The kids get along. We try to keep it light, to not force anything on them. I try to put myself in their shoes, knowing that it can't be easy. Two different homes and now, the occasional sleepover at a third. The emotional impact of seeing your dad with a woman who isn't your mom, or for Elliott seeing his mom with me. We try and tread lightly and move slowly.

On the patio of the boathouse, the crowd of friends and family begin to sing "Happy birthday to you…" Nancy walks toward me with a cake. She places the cake down in front of me and kisses me again. "Aloha" surfboards, palm trees, and… a turtle. I blow out the candles and make a wish: That I never forget this day. This magical moment. The detail. Amidst a demanding work schedule, Elliott's soccer and all her other commitments, Nancy took care of this day with such love and devotion.

"Pops, read my card!" Amelia says.

She sits on my lap and I open her card. She has handwritten a poem that she found on the internet about dads. *Walk a little slower, Dad*. I start to chew the inside of my cheek. Emma is sitting on my other knee. Jesse and Elliott are below, at the lake, fishing.

I am blessed.

CHAPTER 10 — BOYFRIEND SCHOOL

Nancy and I have been dating for just over a year. She's been teaching and I've been learning. The lessons are unspoken. She's never explicit about anything, but I feel she's been ever-so-gently nudging me toward a different kind of manhood.

This summer, for my forty-first birthday, she bought me a chainsaw. She wanted us to clean up her property. And, I think, part of her wanted to see what kind of man she was with. She loves the city but grew up in the country, and I think for her there's a fundamental skill set that I need to have for our relationship to keep growing.

I've done my best to hide my inner nerd from her, but I feel like the jig might be up.

Here's the thing about chainsaws: They're incredibly simple to operate. But the trick with a chainsaw, obviously, is to not tear through one of your body parts, which might sound obvious, but try talking to a doctor from a rural hospital about chainsaw-related emergency room visits. The second trick isn't about the chainsaw but the tree you are trying to cut. I asked an old lumberjack once how a tree would fall and he answered, "wherever she wants." And that's basically the size of it; the tree's going to fall wherever it wants, whether you're standing there or not. And that's not even the most dangerous part.

A little bit of research before I set out on my first tree-felling adventure, and I learn about the barber chair. A tree will sometimes split lengthwise partway through the cut, likely killing, maiming, or otherwise giving a bad headache to whoever happens to be the unlucky operator of the chainsaw. I do this research in private, away from Nancy, because I think it would break her heart to know that she was dating a different kind of guy, one more interested in reading about the invention of the chainsaw than in taking it outside and cutting down that dead tree.

Today is a different lesson. Nancy and I are walking through the narrow streets of the Portobello Road market in London. Notting Hill. The kids are back at school and with their other parents this week, while we have a little romantic getaway.

There are roughly forty different accents in the UK. I lived there for six years. I can reliably differentiate between at least a couple of dozen, but more than the accent: the tone and energy in the voices. Some people think the British are polite and reserved. Those people haven't spent enough time in the pubs along the south coast. I used to work in one. The British I served lived intensely. Closing up on a Friday night sometimes meant picking up crushed glass after a bar fight. But most of the time it was tears of laughter. Jovial and festive, every weekend.

That's the mood in this market. Jovial and festive. Dozens of different accents and throngs of happy people on this West London street. It's fall and the air is crisp but not cold. The market is full of colour. Blue and red storefronts, pink, yellow three-story apartments above. The crowd is a mix of tourists and locals. The stalls lined up and down the street are like a bazaar, full of antiques, old books, and paintings. There's a portly man with a grey flat cap and a Northern accent, speaking and smiling with a shop owner as he walks by. Jolly old chap they all seem familiar with.

Nancy is drawn to some glass doorknobs in one of the stalls. Boxes full of antique doorknobs. I get the sense that she could spend the day here. She fascinates me. Her eye for beauty, for design. I don't think I've ever noticed a doorknob in my life, but she's enthralled, holding them up to the light.

"Do you like this one?" she asks.

"Absolutely. Love it," I say.

I can't tell the difference between any of the last six.

"I didn't know you needed doorknobs," I say.

She looks at me quizzically.

"But I don't."

"Oh," I say, confused.

"They're just really beautiful," she says.

But they're doorknobs.

"Are you tired, sweetie?"

"No, I'm just, uh, wondering if we're going to buy something?" I respond.

I want a transaction. We're in a market. Stalls up and down a narrow street. Londoners milling around. Happy tourists bumping into them. We've been here for a few minutes but the egg timer in my mind is already counting down.

"Buy something?" she says, surprised.

Okay, we're just going to walk and stop at all the stalls. I want to be the best boyfriend I can be. She's teaching me how. This is a learning moment.

I'm good on flights and drives. I'm good at getting somewhere. Once I'm there though, it's not long before I start to itch for the next somewhere. I had to take a psychological exam for work once. Basic logic tests, Rorschach tests where the guy shows me an abstract image and I project something onto it or derive some meaning from it. I passed, inasmuch as I needed to progress my career. At the end though, the shrink asks me if I have a hard time being still. *You might want to have a little dig around that one day. Some people avoid stillness because they have a hard time with what's going on inside themselves.*

With Nancy, I try to be better. I don't want to be still, I want to move forward, but in our relationship it's a form of giving and I want to be the best boyfriend I can be. It's reciprocal. She compromises. The rest of the day was motion. Fish and chips near Covent Garden, a walk around Kensington. Black cabs and red buses. We ended the day at the British Museum.

Inside the museum is one of the largest collections of Egyptian objects this far from the Nile. As much as I love the English, this feels oddly sacrilegious to me. Egypt has been pillaged, robbed of its tombstones, treasures, and history. Humanity's history. I make a mental note to think about that later.

The museum is a beautiful building. Giant stone columns on the outside. An atrium on the inside. The Great Court. Arched steel and glass ceiling over a quadrangle. Nancy is moved by the architecture. I watch her glide through the place. She floats through the light filtering into the great hall. She pauses by the exhibits; the intricacy of the early period jewelry on display. We move. She leads, I follow, and I learn.

#

Back at the hotel, I consider the museums again. The pillaging of Egypt.

Thankfully, some Egyptian history was recorded. Some of the great Greek philosophers were said to have studied in Egypt. Herodotus visited that ancient land and described a culture of deep devotion, rich in holy ritual. Highly differentiated from the barbarians. Strange in some parts, where men wove and women carried loads on their shoulders. But holy. He did not mock their rituals, nor their gods. He saw the parallels, their shared worship.

I like that kind of exploration. *What can I learn from these people and this land?* Alexander the Great went in a different direction: conquest and dominion, the way of the warrior king. He conquered the land and the people and declared himself a god of Egypt. The son of Amun. A god-size king with an army, he reformed religion in his image.

That's been the warrior king's secret: the cunning. The kings understood that you can't kill an idea. Especially if that idea is a religion that can set a person free, liberate their consciousness from the shackles of culture, enterprise, taxes, and warfare. And that's the cunning of the god-king. Not to erase religion but to change it just enough so that the next generation will pay his taxes and fight in his army.

We are still living in the time of the warrior-king.

Fact: the American CEO of a Fortune 500 company is likely to be a full 2.5 inches taller than the average population of men. The same group of 500 powerful companies has only a handful of woman leaders. Similar disparity for political leaders.

There are fifteen thousand nuclear weapons in the world. Controlled by roughly six men. Nearly the power of a star in the hands of a half-dozen septuagenarians with wet testicles. Just 1 percent of the world population controls over half its wealth; the power accrued by kings over millennia of slavery, the oppression of women, and the blood and life of children on the battlefield.

CHAPTER 11 — FATHERHOOD

Nancy and I haven't seen each other for a few weeks since we got back from England. We are having lunch. We date when the kids' schedules line up. It's a daytime date. Soup and a sandwich at a restaurant near her work.

"I'm a little worried about Emma. She had another breakup," I say.

Nancy is sympathetic.

"I tried to have a father-daughter chat with her about dating."

Nancy stops eating. She has a worried look.

"I drew her a chart. It was a wave function. Peaks and troughs of the relationship cycle. The trough is the low point, after a breakup. Then something happens, and you're climbing up the rising slope. You meet someone, you like the way they make you feel. Pretty soon you're on top of this wave: *life is amazing*. Then something happens again and back down you go. I pointed my finger at the place between waves.

You are here."

Nancy is horrified.

"I'm going to give Emma a call," she says.

I've been learning some parenting skills from her. For her, parenting is devotion. She helps Elliott with his homework every night. She makes him dinners and prepares his lunches. She teaches him discipline, hard work. She listens to his trials and tribulations at school. She drives him to and from soccer and saxophone lessons.

For me, parenting has been a small business with cashflow problems and unproductive employees.

"I made her cry again," I tell Nancy. "I just don't know what to do or say... She's so sad."

"Sometimes you don't need to say or do anything. Just be there for her."

Nancy's words make me reflect.

I've been an okay dad. Fatherhood is a skill. I started off not great and I'm working my way toward decent. That means that with my eldest, Emma, I struggled the most. Lost moments, the forgetfulness and inattention. The times when I was too busy thinking about something else.

Emma was born on a hot summer day in Texas. I love the heat, and El Paso in the summertime didn't let me down. Shade is at a premium; cars park under trees and any kind of awning that a driver can find. There are leather, glove-like shoes for dogs, and those without dance across the pavement on their way to the grassy park.

The lead-up to the birth was full of anticipation for me. About how I would feel. How I would change. How fatherhood would profoundly alter my sense of self and perspective. That morning I would rise a boy; by night I would be a man, a father. I would be different. A better version of myself. Redeemed from the follies of my youth. I would instantly be at ease in this world, comfortable, living a life of meaning and purpose. That fundamental irritation with myself would dissipate.

None of that happened.

She was born. Healthy. But where I expected to feel profoundly changed, nothing happened. I felt nothing—no joy, no love. Maybe a mild sense of relief that everything went okay, but other than that—nothing. Except for maybe that same sense of irritation toward myself I've always carried around. In what should have been the most hallowed moment of my life, I felt annoyed at the droning voice of my inner monologue.

In the hours that followed, I napped beside her. She was in a cot, wrapped in the whitest of cotton blankets. It was quiet enough that I could hear her cooing gently. I watched over her, waiting, hoping to feel something. I dozed in and out of sleep.

I woke up to a young man walking into the room. He whispered something that I couldn't make out as he stood over her cot. He wore a nurse's uniform and signalled to me that he was following some kind of procedure and there was no cause for alarm. He reached into the cot and grabbed her foot. With his other hand he used a device to prick the bottom of it.

She began to cry instantly, and suddenly I did feel something. Violence. I started shaking. Rage. He hurt her. This child. My child. It was primal, this feeling. I was struck with the rarest kind of clarity. *I wanted to kill him*. That the only thing that mattered in this world was her well-being. He hurt her. Inside me was a new wellspring of brutality. I wanted to inflict cruelty on this young man. I was frozen with rage.

He wiped the blood from her foot, made a note, and looked at me oddly. He smiled a confused grin. He motioned that I could pick her up.

In my arms, she cried gently, then cooed, then slept. She was sleeping in my arms. This child. This, miracle. My rage subsided. It wasn't a feeling; it was a change. I was changed. I would never remember what life was like before she was in it. There was only one way for the universe to exist and it was with her at the very centre of it. She radiated her innocence, her tender-hearted peace. She had arrived from a place unknown and now, in my arms, she was my ward.

Since then, I've made her cry far too many times. Of all the shitty feelings a man can have, making your firstborn daughter cry has to be up there at the top. It's never intentional, but that doesn't matter. For her it might as well be.

When she lost her first tooth, it was a big deal. I wanted to make it a big deal. She brought it to me and flashed a big-gapped smile.

"We need to get a certificate for the tooth fairy," I said to her.

She sat on my knee while we searched the internet for an appropriate document of authenticity. The printer came to life. She scrawled her name on the paper. I signed mine. We folded it up and placed it along with the tooth in a ziplock bag.

That night, we placed it under the pillow. I kissed her on the forehead. She slept.

I woke up the next morning. She was standing over me. Holding back tears.

"The... the... tooth ferry... the tooth ferry... didn't come," she cried and handed me the plastic ziplock.

Shit. I completely forgot the most important part. I took her in my arms.

"Sweetie, the tooth fairy has twenty-four hours. Let's give her a few more hours," I said, hoping I could make it up to her.

Moments of inattention lost to time forever. A signal to my child that this phone, this email, this thing I have going in my head is so much more important than you. *You don't matter, this does.* For a long time, at some level, I believed that devotion just meant paying the bills on time and showing up for the big moments—the graduation and the school plays. I'm learning that with Emma, it's about rebuilding trust, that I can be there for her, not with a solution, just actually there, present. I'm learning this from watching Nancy. The way she lives. The way she loves. Her presence and devotion.

"How's your soup?" she asks.

I look at her strangely.

"Are you okay?" she asks.

I hear her asking me something but I'm in a daze. She's so beautiful. I can't stop looking at her. *She's teaching me how to love.* I'm staring at her. This is getting awkward but I can't seem to move my head or eyes.

"Oh, sorry, yes. The soup," I say.

A few thoughts are whizzing around my head. A few seconds ago, in a part of my mind I decided to propose to her. Now I'm wondering if I should bring this idea up as a concept for us to discuss together or if

I should wait and actually propose. We never spoke about marriage. I have no idea how she feels about the possibility of a second marriage. I didn't know how I felt about it either until a few seconds ago.

Feels like the mature thing to do is to ask how she feels about marriage as an institution. If this is even a place she might want to take our relationship.

But I don't broach the subject.

"The soup is, really good. Yeah, it's really good. Great, actually! I love it! How's yours? Do you like it? It looks really good! We probably should get back though, right? What time do you have to be at work?" I say.

She looks at me strangely now. I look for the waiter. We need to go. I need to see her dad.

CHAPTER 12 — REINDEER

I meet Nancy's dad at McDonalds just after the noon rush. He's sitting at a table, glasses on and reading the paper. Silver hair and soft eyes, Nancy's dad is a happy guy. He reminds me of my grandad. Curious, engaged with the affairs of the world, but not really all that opinionated.

"Alec!" he exclaims when he sees me. He pronounces my name the same way my grandad used to. It makes me smile every time.

He shakes my hand vigorously. He's a strong but gentle man and from the same part of the country my grandad came from. Similar values and temperament.

"How's your business doing?" he asks.

"Going well, things are solid," I tell him. So much of my life is business. With friends and family, I generally try to steer clear of the subject, but Nancy's dad is so proud and happy. He delights in any good news I can share.

"Any new contracts in far-off places?" he asks.

"A few. Southeast Asia mostly. Singapore and Hong Kong."

"Incredible." He folds his paper.

I smile. I feel warm inside anytime I'm around him.

"You probably wondered why we couldn't talk on the phone?" I say.

"I did. When my wife asked why I was going to meet you, I just told her *I don't know*."

"Well, then let me end the suspense. I wanted to meet you here to ask for your daughter's hand in marriage."

He flashes a bright smile.

"Did you ask her already?" he asks.

"No, no I didn't."

"Does she know you're asking me?"

"No, no she doesn't."

"She doesn't know you're going to ask?"

"I didn't know myself until recently."

"What do you think she will say?"

"I have no idea. I've only planned up to the moment of me asking her to marry me."

He smiles and pats me on the back.

"Well in that case, good luck!" he says.

I'm following my heart. The analyst in me wants to know the outcome. Plan things out, do whatever I can to improve the odds and make it a winning proposal. My heart slaps the analyst in the back of the head. *Follow me and stop talking.*

#

I'm still in bed. Nancy left less than half an hour ago but she's already calling me. I'm groggy.

"It's me. I hit the car," she says.

"Wait, what?" I ask. "Are you okay?"
"Yes. Yes, of course, but I scratched your car! I'm so sorry… I sent you pictures."

"Okay, but you're okay?" I ask.

"Yes, sweetie! Better than okay! I'm so happy!" she says.

"All right, sweetness. As long as you're okay, there's nothing to worry about."

"Okay, bye!" Click and she's gone.

I proposed to her yesterday. I was on bended knee, by the lake where I hoped we could one day build a life together, and I asked her to marry me.

I'm looking at the photos she just sent. *Jesus, that's not a scratch.* The entire back bumper is caved in! But I'm laughing. She sounded so happy on the phone giving me the news. She's happy. Happy in a way that made her completely oblivious to the warning sound the car made when she was reversing near a cement pillar. And I couldn't care less about the car right now, because I'm just as happy as she is. Maybe even happier, because something I did had given her such unqualified and unmitigated joy. To be a cause of someone else's happiness is a pretty cool feeling.

We drove up to the lake yesterday. There was frost in the fields but not yet snow. I had in my pocket a ruby that a jeweler friend had found for me at the gem market. I'd wanted a ruby, because Nancy loves colour. It was a beautiful stone, a special kind, untreated, with a shade varying between red and pink. Another friend of mine had helped me set the ruby in a plastic ring. It was a child's Christmas toy ring, a reindeer with a red ruby nose. We'd placed it in a wooden box. I wanted to give Nancy a ring, but I wanted her to design it first, to make it hers, to endow it with her talent for creating beauty.

I had hinted on the ride down that I wanted to give her an early Christmas present. That it was the kind that couldn't fit under the Christmas tree and that we'd need to store it for the winter. She suspected it was a paddleboard and I had fed that suspicion.

I was nervous on the drive down. We had never spoken of marriage. Her dad knew, as well as my children and a few close friends, but nobody else. I had no idea how she would react, or what I would say if my proposal was rejected.

We got to the lake. I parked. I asked her to close her eyes. I held her hand and walked her to the backwoods, near the stream. The air was cool but not icy; we were warmed by the midday sun. The ground was covered in leaves. The stream was not yet frozen. We were alone, in nature, on what was for me the most hallowed ground in the world—the site where my grandparents lived out their dreams of family.

She stood before me, eyes closed, smiling in anticipation. I rustled an old tarp nearby like I was unveiling a paddleboard. Then I got down on one knee, pulled the wooden box out of my pocket, and opened it.

"You can open your eyes now," I said.

She did and was silent. Her expression stayed the same. She was frozen.

I began to speak but fumbled my words. Something about her beauty and wanting to spend the rest of my life with her.

She did not speak and her expression did not change. She made a gesture for me to get up and she put her arms around me. I felt her heart racing. I felt my heart racing. I still had no idea what she was going to say. We held each other for what felt like an eternity until finally, I broke the silence.

"Um… do you have an answer?" I asked tentatively.

"Oh my God, I thought I already answered! Yes! My answer is yes!"

I smiled. I was still holding the box. She had not even seen the reindeer ring. I put it in her hand. She was confused until she looked closer at the reindeer nose. "Oh my God… It's so beautiful!"

She was happy. Over-the-moon happy. Her words were scattered and excited. I soaked it all in. Her happiness, the woods, my wet knee imprinted with moss and leaf. The stream. The stillness of the lake. She examined the ring and I examined the moment. I was grateful. Somehow, someway, with the help of friends, I had made this moment sacred.

The drive back was punctuated with waves of excitement and joy. There was one more question that I had not yet asked. I was waiting for the right moment. It was a complicated question, and even though I didn't care about the answer I felt it important to ask. It had to do with a debt I felt toward my grandparents. Something I wanted to at least try and repay.

"Will you take my last name? I know how much trouble it is and how old-fashioned and you don't have to... it's not that—"

"Shhhhh... I would be honoured to take your last name," she answered.

I was blown away. I didn't think either of us was particularly traditional, and in our culture, a woman taking a man's last name is probably more of a scarlet letter than a badge of pride. But this was going to be the second time around for us, and I think we wanted to try it a different way. The way my grandparents and her parents did it. We would opt for the traditional path, right down to the church wedding.

The next twenty-four hours were a blur of phone calls and goodwill. Her dad was still in suspense and bursting at the seams with the secret, and I asked her to call him first. Then we called our children, my parents, the friends who had helped me and knew of my plans, her friends, our community. They were unequivocally happy. Our unity was their blessing. Our little corner of the world would be blessed by our coming together as one.

#

I call Fadi.

"Brother, I'm getting married!" I tell him.

"Finally! Congratulations!" he says.

While I was taking boyfriend lessons last year, Fadi left the company. After over a decade of working together, he moved to Dubai. He's working for a large corporation now. It wasn't a completely spontaneous decision. It took the whole weekend before the idea came into his head and he put the For Sale sign up on his home. I was sad to see him leaving but admired the courage, to take a risk and make a change.

"What about you? How's your love life?" I ask.

"I'm dating someone. Might be getting serious."

"How long you guys been dating?"

"Two weeks."

I'm laughing.
"What's so funny?"

"Nothing, man, just don't ever change."

CHAPTER 13 — OLD CHURCH

It's been over a year since we got engaged. Almost two, actually. Between work and the kids, time just kind of flew by. Nancy and I are going over photos and drawings of the cottage renovations we are planning.

We are making plans, setting priorities, working out styles. It's our third renovation project in two years. First my home, then the office, and now the cottage, a place where we hope we can share a common family life. A place where everyone we care about can meet, relax, and enjoy each other's company. My hope is that it will be filled with as many stories and warm memories and grandkids as the house my grandad built.

The renovations have brought some tensions into our relationship. We generally share the same values and goals, but we approach the changes from two different directions. For Nancy, it's about design aesthetic whereas for me it's all about function. When she showed me the preliminary plans for the cottage, I noted there weren't any toilets. She hesitated. I could see her wrestling with her thoughts. *There was nothing beautiful about a toilet; was there a way to do away with them altogether?* In all fairness, my design would probably include urinals.

We generally meet in the middle, where form meets function. But each decision brings with it a little fatigue. There are fifty different shades of white. We need to pick one. Each shade has different finishes. I prefer eggshell she prefers flat. We compromise on flat. The disagreements accumulate.

"Baby, what's wrong?" I ask.

She's not enthusiastic about the new plans. I thought she'd be excited.

"Nothing," she says curtly.

"Okay, so that's not true. Do you want to talk about it or just leave it alone?" I ask.

"Let's just go through the plans," she says.

"There's no rush on the design. We don't have to do any of this now. Why don't we just enjoy the summer and look at this again in the fall," I offer.

And she bursts into tears.

"Baby, what's going on?" I plead.

"We're never going to get married... You said you wanted to get married at the cottage and it'll be another year before it's ready."

"Oh no. Wait, we don't have to get married at the cottage. We can get married anywhere we want."

"I want to get married at the cottage," she says.

"Okay, so let's just do it before the renovations. We can get a tent or something..."

"I don't want a tent."

Nancy is the most reasonable and rational person I have ever met. Her mind is brilliant. Her soul is on fire. She's completely balanced, in touch with herself and communicates with clarity—99.99 percent of the time.

In case this happens to be the rare occasion of murkiness, I wade carefully. I hold her hand.

"What's the matter?" I ask.

"We've been engaged for over a year and we don't have a wedding date. Do you really need to ask me this question?"

"Okay. Then let's set a date."

"I don't want to set a date now. I don't want to be pushing you into this."

Nancy.

"You're not pushing me into anything. I want this as much, if not more than you do. Honestly, I thought with everything going on, planning a wedding would just be more stress than we could handle but, baby, I don't care when or where, let's just get married. Should we do it this summer?"

"I like the idea of a winter wedding," she says.

"Okay, so this winter... Just after Christmas, on the weekend before the kids go back to school."

She checks her diary.

"January sixth?"

"Done!"

"We just need to find a church."

#

I'm leaning on a rake by the fire at the cottage. I'm waiting for Nancy to get back from two different Sunday masses. She's choosing our church.

I'm hoping she chooses my village church. It's only a five-minute drive from here but there are some good reasons for her not to pick it. *Rundown* might be a generous description. Somewhere between dilapidated and condemned might be more accurate. Apparently, there are still services there, but I never notice any activity whenever I drive by.

I was baptized there. There are pictures of me as a baby, my family standing around me, the priest standing over me. The church was full. Not for me, but because it was full every Sunday. I just happened to be the baby the entire village was celebrating that week.

Growing up, we went to that church every Sunday over the summer. My grandparent, parents, aunts, uncles, and cousins. Everyone who couldn't fake an injury or find some other way of getting out of going. We dressed up. Ties on the men and boys, skirts and dresses for the ladies. I don't remember a single sermon, just the clock. I knew the timing of the different rituals and could count down exactly how long from when everyone shook hands exchanging peace to when I'd be back outside playing.

I don't know if my family was the first to stop going, but it seemed like within the space of a few years, the parking lot went from full to empty. The church, on the corner at the centre of the village, went from the beating heart of a thriving community to a skeletal reminder of a bygone era.

Nancy is smiling when she pulls into the driveway. She gets out of the car and walks toward the fire.

"I found our church!" she says.

"Which one did you pick?"

"The one in the village. It's going to be a job to get it ready, but I loved the priest."

"Really? That's great."

I wasn't sure if Nancy would be into the church wedding when I asked. Feels like we are both a little tentative but curious about a religious ceremony.

"I spoke to him after the service. I gave him our situation. There won't be any problem. We just need to take some preparatory lessons with him leading up to the ceremony. Is that okay?"

"Can't wait!" I respond.

She laughs.

"Your face... your face is full of ash," she says and kisses me.

#

It was hard not to instantly like Father Olivier when I met him the first time. He was a joy to be around. He loved love—it was his life's work, his passion. Helping shepherd couples toward deeper unity lit him up inside. He laughed easily and had an uncanny ability to select the exact topic that we needed to talk about at that very moment in our relationship.

Our first meeting was in the back of the church, the room behind the altar. The winter cold was setting in. We had on toques and mittens.

"Today… today is about sex!" he said, throwing his head back with a hearty laugh.

Nancy and I looked at each other with curiosity and a certain amount of awkwardness. Unless my dear Cameroonian brother was about to share some unknown tips and tricks from the motherland, I wasn't sure how useful our talk was going to be today. This was our first marriage in the church, but the second marriage for each of us, and besides, we were born in the '70s and came of age in the '80s. Feels like human sexuality has been covered, written about, rapped about, and filmed and photographed from every conceivable angle. Literally.

"Often couples come to me with problems. Irritations. Blockages to love…" he began saying. "I stop and ask them: Have you made love recently?" He roared with laughter again.

"Like you, they are stunned that a man of the cloth is speaking of sexuality, or uncomfortable that a man devoted to celibacy can speak of such things," he continued with a broad smile. "But, so often, their answer is no... no, they have not made love recently. Sometimes they cannot even remember the last time they were in union."

Nancy looked discreetly in my general direction. We'd been busy. Renovations, wedding planning, work, kids, travel. Cold weather and the vaguest irritation with one another. Neither of us quite feeling romantic enough at exactly the same time.

"I send them home. Go find one another, I say, and if you still have problems, call me again and come see me, and we will talk more. They almost never come back." He laughed again.

"Nancy, you are a devoted mother. Alex, you are a devoted father. You both work hard. I can see your passion for the world, I can feel your ambitions, you have told me about your plans... but you must make time for your love. You must not take each other for granted. Alex, you must make the time to woo Nancy. Nancy, you must make the effort to seduce Alex. You both must make time to love each other and to feel your unity... It is the only thing you must do, because from this union everything else will flow—the kids' well-being, your work, your ambitions—they will all flow from a place of unity." He wasn't laughing anymore. He was earnest.

I saw in him then the intense beauty of devotion. A man so committed to love and union that he would devote his entire being to a life without it. I felt, though, that the union this man sought in this world was simply of a different kind. He was seeking union with divinity. A complete circuit of ethereal light between him and God. Source, sink, and current flowing intensely through the channel. He could never fully love another person romantically, not in the way he loved the divine.

I asked him once what drew him into the clergy, and he told me a story of his childhood. In his native Cameroon, he had attended a school run by the sisters, the nuns of some Catholic order. He saw something in them. He liked being around them. One day after class he asked his teacher if he could walk with her, and together they walked. They spoke little. He followed her to what she described as her calling; teaching was her profession, but helping children was her calling, so he followed her to a clinic for visually impaired children. He watched her help, nurture, heal, and lighten the hearts of these children who could not see the world of beauty he took for granted. He was inspired. His heart was set and his decision was made.

His parents were devastated. His was a family of aspiring engineers and doctors, teachers and managers. His spiritual aspirations were, for them, negative. He would accrue no wealth. He would father no offspring, have no influence or power. Just grace. Magic. As far as his parents were concerned their kid believed in magic, and this was the worst possible news.

At the seminary he studied hard, he was devoted. But here the structure and hierarchy of the church began to sadden him. There were no blind children; no poor or sick to help. Just rules. Pages upon pages of books and volumes of rules and strange manuscripts. He persevered, but his doubt festered. Early one day he sat alone by the sea, contemplating his future. He questioned his path. He prayed for a sign from the heavens. And he cried. He was afraid. He was verging on a lifelong commitment and not yet twenty years old.

A man came up alongside him. It was an elder priest from the seminary. The old man sat down on the beach next to him. Olivier wiped away his tears, and for a while there was silence. Only the sound of the waves breaking onto the beach. Finally the old man broke the silence. He put his hand on Olivier's shoulder and spoke softly.

"We never really know, do we?" he said.

Olivier was ordained. He became Father Olivier. His passion evolved from helping children to helping their parents, too. He continued to learn. He came to Canada for school. Modern Western psychology and sociology and ancient mystic texts came together in his mind, and his calling became clearer. He would help heal the world one couple at a time.

Today is our last meeting before the ceremony. We meet in the rectory. It's a small room. The walls are painted institutional blue. The paint is chipped and peeling. It's cold. Our breath is fogging the air. The starting point is always a biblical passage, which always precipitates in me a kind of mental resistance and anxiety. I get a little irritated around the Bible. I get uncomfortable around any kind of mental rigidity and especially zealotry... of any kind. A rational scientist preaching atheism or a proselytizing religious person feel the same to me. Rigid. Unfounded certainty.

For some people, the Bible inspires: love, beauty, and wisdom. Usually for me it's something else: politics, power, judgment, and division. I'm hopeful today it's going to be the former.

And so I sit, quiet and tense, beside Nancy in this rundown church with frozen air and Père Olivier guiding us toward a lifetime commitment.

Nancy envelops my clenched fist with her delicate hand. Père Olivier begins to speak gently. The verse is about submission. Something about the woman who submits herself to the man. Suddenly her hand tightens around mine and the hairs on the back of my neck stand to attention. This is about to get awkward.

"Wives, submit yourself to your own husbands, as unto the Lord."

Ohhh shit.

Nancy is an aerospace engineer. She is strong. She has fought and won her independence. She's a proud mom. She's an upstanding citizen. She is in every way equal to, if not greater than, both men in this pale, dilapidated room. She is being asked obliquely to submit herself to me, her future husband—as defective a man as has ever been. A man who stumbled through his own life only to fall ass-backward into hers at a moment of sublime weakness.

Lucky? Yes. Worthy? No.

"For the husband is the head of the wife, even as Christ is the head of the Church, and he is the saviour of the body."

My hand is white with tension. Her fingers squeeze my knuckles.

"Therefore, as the Church is subject unto Christ, so let the wives be to their own husbands in everything."

I want to get out of here. Who wrote this gobbledygook? Christ wasn't married, right? Bunch of unmarried bachelors wrote this? Sexless nerds with scrolls and sandals?

"Husbands, love your wives even as Christ also loved the Church and gave himself for it."

Nancy's hand is relaxing slightly. Father Olivier is gentle, even if the words are harsh. Maybe the translation is wonky. Maybe there is a flower of wisdom growing somewhere in these weeds.

"For this cause shall a man leave his father and mother and shall be joined unto his wife and they two shall be one flesh."

More church stuff but I'm starting to relax a little. Not because of the words, but because I'm here with Nancy and Father Olivier. There is a peace in this cold room that I'm starting to feel. We wanted the church wedding, we hoped for the mysticism, the sacred, and I guess this is part of it. I'm all in for this woman. But somehow I don't feel worthy.

I am not worthy of her submission.

I am not worthy.

I whisper it out loud. "I am not worthy." Slowly, again. "I am not worthy," and her hand relaxes. My back straightens and I see a vision of this woman, walking alone, fiercely buffeted by the winds of this world, determined. She can get there alone. She can get through anything. I just don't want her to. I don't want her to exert herself doing anything I can do for her. I don't want her to lose her independence either; I don't want to possess her. I just want to be beside her. I want to love her.

For a moment there is a silent tension in the room.

I realize something important. I cannot take her. I cannot coerce, manipulate, or dominate her. I can only hope, with great humility, that she will submit herself to my love, protection, and care. I cannot love her unless she allows me to. Her submission is an act of great tenderness, an opening into the deepest kind of vulnerability. Most of all, for me, a belief that somehow I am able to be the kind of man worthy of that submission, a precious gift to me that only I can cherish. It is her measure of this man that I can only strive to become, her gift that fuels my desire to grow strong enough to accept it.

"Will you let me love and cherish you?" I ask.

She looks at me with tender eyes.

"Oui," she says.

My fist unclenches and our hands fold together. Father Olivier smiles gently. The room is silent again, but this time without my tension. There is a kind of tranquility and slowness to the moment.

CHAPTER 14 — GRACE

It is the coldest day of the year. Colder than on parts of Mars. I am
outside the church in a tuxedo shovelling snow from the stairs. I run
inside every few minutes to warm my face and ears. The church
has been transformed into a winter wonderland. Garlands of pine,
Christmas trees, woollen blankets over all the pews. The cracks on
the walls are covered with mistletoe. My old church, revitalized and
renewed by Nancy's touch.

She spent months preparing for this moment. She turned this special
day into something else. Something sacred. She went shopping with
Emma and Amelia. Emerald-green bridesmaid dresses. She bought
tartan ties and pocket squares for the groomsmen—our two boys and
her father. She organized her friends into teams for flowers, music,
and food and made a very short list for me. The kind of list you pin to
a child's jacket on the first day of school.

Our friends and family begin to show up and the day blurs into a
field of colours and feelings. Nancy's love and devotion appear in
the details. The horse-drawn sleigh waiting outside the church after

the ceremony. The miniature ponies for the young bridesmaids. The pictures by the snow fields and waterfall.

Her dress has an antique theme to match the decor. The bridesmaids wear tartan shells over their dresses. A professional singer rings out "Ave Maria." Early afternoon sunlight filters through stained glass windows, glowing shades and shadows of saints dancing in the icy air. And despite the cold, there is a warmth to the day. Dozens of close friends and family in the pews share blankets, huddled and together.

I once had a problem with the concept of kneeling before God, because it made me think of servitude and subservience. Mike changed my notion: "It's not for God, man, it's for you. For you to push your ego out of the way just long enough to feel grace." And I do. I feel the grace of the moment, of Nancy and of everyone around us rooting for our bond to grow strong and withstand the tests of time. On my knees, I am graced with the humility to see and feel it all, for my heart to swell with gratitude and profound joy.

The party afterward is a blur of tartan, roaring fire, laughter, dancing, and love. Her dad toasts us succinctly, with a tear in his eye and a lump in his throat. He raises his glass and says, "There is nothing more precious than to love and to be loved in return." Emma speaks from her notes and makes the room laugh and cry.

I speak about a photo I came across once, the image of a woman. In the photo she has her back to the camera, walking toward the vague outline of a mountain; her hair is dark and windswept and her arm is outstretched behind her, offering to pull you along into her world. That's how I feel about Nancy. She pulled me into her world of beauty and love, and I don't ever want to leave.

Nancy speaks that night with such emotion. It is a whirlwind of love, gratitude, and tenderness. She is overwhelmed. She is happy. And the knowledge that I'm a part of that is an amazing feeling.

Père Olivier joins us that evening. He dances and laughs and eats heartily along with everyone else. He loves life. He loves love. And I have learned a lot from him.

I can go over the day backward and forward in my mind and still feel the richness of its texture and depth. If anything, my appreciation for the details and the occasion expands. A sacred moment in an old church.

#

Nancy and I are standing outside in the dark. We are in Siem Reap, Cambodia. Across the small lake is the faint outline of Angkor Wat, one of the world's oldest religious temples. We are waiting to watch the sun rise over the temple.

Our honeymoon started in Hong Kong. I had been there often for business. It was Nancy's first time there, and I wanted to see it again through her eyes. We passed through Singapore and Malaysia and finally Cambodia. The honeymoon was full of new cultures and experiences, but it is Cambodia that opened our hearts.

Cambodians have lived through twin tragedies of war and genocide. In the cities and villages, most people are under sixty, having been babies or young children during the time of the Killing Fields. It feels like the people share a deep unspoken connection.

The sun rises and we take in the splendor of the Capital of Temples. The water features and lush landscape around the grounds. The grandeur and symmetry of the towers lit by the morning sun. We walk through the gardens toward the entrance. The bas-relief carvings along the walls, *so much precise craftsmanship*. Geometric art of the grandest scale; even if we could, we wouldn't reproduce it today. I don't think we aspire in quite the same way that people did back then.

Angkor Wat stands apart from any temple, cathedral, mosque, or monument I've ever seen. Architecturally, it makes the Vatican seem unambitious, almost petty. I'm not knocking Michelangelo; I just don't think he ever saw Angkor Wat. But it's about more than just the buildings. The atmosphere, the walls, the carved stones, the vivid representations of female figures—in the innermost spaces of the temple I only see carvings of women—the sensation of walking around the place is deeply moving. There is a presence here, a distinctly feminine quality, like nothing I have ever felt before.

From Siem Reap, we travel southeast toward Phnom Penh. Along the way we visit the elephants at a wildlife sanctuary deep in the country. It's run by a non-profit group specifically for injured wildlife. It is our first time seeing elephants. In the long car ride to the sanctuary, our guide tells us the story of the elephant that chased the monkey who had stolen the bananas, the monkey swinging from tree to tree and the elephant flattening each tree in pursuit. He tells stories about the animals' intelligence, how willingly the injured elephants allow themselves to be helped. One of the elephants had lost a foot to a trap, so her prosthetic had to be removed and her stump cleaned twice daily.

We watch the caretaker and the elephant. They have developed a code involving clicks that allow the two to collaborate. We watch the man and the elephant working together. A few clicks and she raises her maimed leg. He removes the leather straps from the prosthetic. He cleans it. Cleans her stump and reattaches the prosthetic. A few more clicks and some bananas. The man is so devoted. So gentle. And she seems *grateful*.

It is incredible to look into her eyes and feel a connection; to touch her skin, and to feel her touch mine; to swing her trunk to my arm so she can feel who I am.

People talk about projecting personality onto animals— anthropomorphism. Something *dumb* feels intelligent, they say, because we project ourselves onto what we see. My guess is that these people have not spent much time with elephants. For a moment, caring for them—their well-being and protection—seems like the most natural and important thing we could ever do. The idea of killing one of these creatures simply for its tusks feels as absurd as killing an artist for one of their molars. Insane. The idea of enslaving them for labor or driving them out of the wild to build a movie theatre and a McDonald's, the height of profanity and the depths of folly. In the moment we are with them a sense of clarity emerges in me: *We are the stewards and caretakers of this world.* That's us. That's our job.

Three weeks of matrimonial bliss, and then on the last day I feel a sudden sense of dread. The honeymoon is over and we are headed home. Something about heading back into the reality that is waiting for me back home. Nothing specifically about my own life but rather the world I am heading back into.

This sense that we are living on borrowed time, on inherited wealth and freedom. It's a febrile period; a lot of excess heat in the system. A lot of volatility in streets around the world. In high offices, too.

I feel a sense of urgency, that the centre isn't holding and something needs to change before it's too late. The fires of the world are not yet raging at their full force, but if we don't bring the centre together soon, we're in for a blazing inferno.

PART II – The Shaman

The camel spoke to me too. And he said, "Wow you look lost. What's a guy like you doing in the desert?"

CHAPTER 15 — OUTSIDE TIME

Somewhere in this story, I don't even know when. I was on a plane. I exchanged some stories with the man beside me. He asked if I was a Trustafarian. I'd never heard the term. I looked it up. I was horrified. No sir! I wanted to say, I'm a responsible suburban house husband who works hard, drives his kids to school every day, and pays his taxes. Except it wasn't true anymore. Any of it. I said goodbye to my kids and parents to search for something I cannot even name.

One year before the pandemic.

Einstein famously said that time is an illusion, albeit a stubbornly persistent one. I never really appreciated the profundity of the statement until now.

I am presently outside time. My body is somewhere else. In more familiar terms, it's lying on a thin mat, in a house somewhere near London. The shamanic ceremony started a few hours ago. Referring to my body, I say 'it' because right now, I don't feel any particular attachment to the flesh-covered and marrow-filled skeletal structure lying on a mat somewhere inside time. My consciousness has become unbound and I'm hanging out in eternity. God is waving and telling me to say hi, y'all.

Turns out, even in eternity I still have all my faculties. I have a perspective. I just have a little more freedom of movement, of attention and focus. I can't really describe this place, except by a new contrast: I see my body now, *my life*, as a raft drifting downstream in a small rivulet of time; gently floating down a one-way tributary of entropy, moment by moment flowing toward the great unknown.

Except it's not unknown to me anymore, it's just unknowable. I'm here now, in the source and the sink. It's the place where nothing ever started and everything has always ended. I know that doesn't make logical sense, but bear with me. That which is outside time also is outside of language. But I'll do my best to share how I got here.

First, a gentle caveat: I am not an 'outside time' kind of guy. Nancy and I have been married for a couple of years. There's a sense of normalcy to life. And more than enough fun and adventure inside time. We don't have room in our little world for whimsy and magic. We are actually midway through a move to the Middle East. While my body is over there sweating, she would have just landed in Dubai. I'll be joining her next week, right after I find my way back to my body.

It's a business move for me. A career move for her. The kids have grown up. At college or on their way. We have a three-year plan. It's rational. We wrote it down. Worked out a lot of details. Pros/Cons.

Contingencies. Wills. Nowhere on the plan did I write down visiting a shaman, leaving my body and hanging out in eternity. My bad.

So, how I got here. Well, once upon a time there was an election that changed everything...

CHAPTER 16 — ELECTION NIGHT

Nancy and I are in bed, with the TV on. It's a special night; the first time we've had a date night in a long time. Between getting married, soccer, hockey, renovations, work, and travel it feels like we've been rolling down a never-ending hill.

We've covered some miles together. Whenever I've traveled to a nice place for work, Nancy's been able to join me for an extended weekend. We've been to Malta, Greece, New York City. I finally got to show her the turtles in Maui. We even took the kids there. I watched from the beach while they all took surfing lessons.

"What time do the results come in?" she asks.

"I think they start around eight p.m.," I reply.

She's excited. She's prepared a glass of white wine and a small bowl of potato chips, the same ritual as Oscar night.

"I can't believe it's happening!" she says.

It's the first time the US will elect a woman to the highest office. It's not a foregone conclusion, but it's a safe bet.

"The world is going to change!" she says.

The TV newscaster is showing maps of colour. Numbers. Percentages of population. Racial, age, and gender breakdowns. There is a buzz. Like the Olympics, the US presidential election is a global event. Part pageantry, part spectacle, watched by people around the world with curiosity, and for Nancy right now, a kind of delight.

This year it's unusual because of the first woman presidential candidate and the idea that there will be a 'first gentleman' in the White House. It's also a little strange because her opponent is not a politician. People call him a businessman. I've lived in the business world most of my life and he strikes me more like a grifter than an entrepreneur. The guy on a New York City street corner playing Three Card Monte with tourists for five dollars a game.

I'm a sucker for the well-crafted grift. I've been on the wrong side of a hustle more times than a grown man should. Last Christmas I bought a stereo system from a guy in a parking lot. When I showed the kids my amazing deal, Emma burst out laughing. "You got hustled!" she said and showed me the internet hustle of stereos in parking lots. It was a $5 speaker in a $10 shiny box. There's a saying about a fool and his money. I paid a lot more than $15 and let's just leave it at that. A part of me did know it was a hustle, but I played it through. Everyone knows the magician isn't real, but sometimes it's nice to make believe for a while, to plant the magic beans just to see what happens.

"She's leading!" Nancy says.

The polls are starting to come in and Hillary Clinton is building up a decent lead. But a few states on the East Coast are saying the race is too close to call, which is a little surprising.

Nancy and I have never discussed politics. Not for any philosophical reason; I just don't think either of us have particularly strong views about any one thing. Nancy's strongest opinions are usually about the beauty of a thing, a moment or person. Integrity and dignity. Compassion. People looking out for one another, and the striving, the incredible feats where a person rises up against all odds.

Lately, she's been reading the Nobel Prize–winning book about a young woman from Pakistan. Malala, Nobel Prize Laureate. She's inspired by her struggle, her love, and her leadership. And for Nancy tonight, it's not a political event but a moral one. A capstone on centuries, millennia even, of struggle for women to share in the power and burden of governing.

"What's happening?" she asks.

"I think he's is doing better than people expected," I say.

He's over-performing the polls.

"You think he might win?"

"I don't think so," I say. "She still has strong support in the West. Michigan and a few other states will probably fall her way."

I'm apolitical for various reasons. My trade for the past twenty years has been technology—systems, logic. I'm a student of systems: how they work, how they break, how to build better ones. I've developed some theories, some intuitions about design principles, what works and what doesn't. In building a company, raising capital, integrating into a wider corporate ecosystem and then a global one, I began applying these design principles and this system view to organizations, people, and eventually government.

Dynamic systems grow and after a while they become unwieldy, inefficient, and unpredictable. The knobs and buttons on the console don't work in the way that anyone understands. It's an uncomfortable truth, and when it happens in large technology projects, managers and engineers tend to dance around it for a little before the project caves in on itself. When it happens to governments, the dance lasts for generations, apparently.

What is true for software is true for business and government. And the answer is always the same: refactoring and redesign. Western democracy 2.0. Systemic reform is the only issue that should be at the top of a ticket. Who leads that reform is less important than the coalition of everyday citizens that need to devote themselves to the problem of untangling a complicated web. The good news, the really good news, is that the kind of democratic systems that can be created in 2020 are orders of magnitude more efficient than whatever could have been conceived of in the 1700s. Freer, fairer, more engaging and empowering. The bad news: It's not the kind of story with heroes or villains that will sell a newspaper, and few people are paying attention to the underlying problems.

"I can't believe it… I don't understand," she says mournfully.

I try holding her hand but she pulls it away. She's raging. Somehow, this evening feels like a competition between male and female, which is silly and I want no part of it. I stay quiet.

"How could anybody—" She cuts herself off.

I didn't think I had a horse in this race. But now, feeling Nancy's utter disappointment and sad resignation, the night feels like a major failure. A missed opportunity, and more, an unsettling turning point. Less about the guy winning and more about the times. US elections can sometimes be cultural milestones. Ways of measuring the progression of Western culture.

Tonight doesn't feel like progression to me. It's something else. A feeling in my gut, that primordial place that senses danger before my mind can process it. If the world wasn't already there, tonight will seal it. We are entering a period of high knowledge, great power, and low wisdom.

#

I'm sitting with Mike inside the diner. There's a foot of snow outside. Inside, the natural gas fireplace warms the room. There's a plate of half-eaten nachos and chicken wing bones on the table. Mike ate the wings. I ate the nachos. He's doing a keto diet.

I take a small tablet out of a plastic tube and put it under my tongue.

"You still taking those?" he asks.

"The Nicorette? Beats smoking."

"It's been over a year," he says.

"Thanks for keeping track. I've doubled up since the election. How'd Anne take it?"

"We didn't watch. I've been telling her for months that he would get elected. I don't think she could handle me being right on the same night as the election. People just want simple. He keeps it simple."

"You're not worried?" I ask.

"About what?"

"Speaking simply and managing complexity are two different skill sets," I say.

"It'll be fine."

Mike's unfounded assuredness irritates me.

"Buddy, we just put a grifter in charge of the free world. You think this is all going to work out okay?" I say.

"Who's this 'we'?"

"Us, humans, our era. We're screwed, man," I say.

"You always worry about stuff you have no control over. You make things bigger than they need to be. The US had an election. In four years, there will be another one, and again and again."

"That's not a natural law. Evolution… physics… Life doesn't care about something somebody wrote down."

"What are you saying?" he asks.

"I'm not sure, but the status quo is officially over."

"So put that on a sandwich board and go walk around downtown. What do you want to do?"

"Find wisdom."

"You want to go to Tibet?"

"I don't know where to find it. I read something about some tribes in the Amazon that have ceremonies to connect people to God or deep consciousness or wisdom or whatever word you want to use."

"You want to dance around a fire and change the world?"

"No. I just want to understand my own role. I don't know what to do anymore, other than keep making money. Roasting marshmallows while the world burns doesn't feel like the right play."

"The world isn't burning. Stop watching TV or change the channel. Take the kids to a movie or something."

It is literally burning, Mike.

"Seriously though, the shaman ceremony. I think it's legit. You want to come with me?"

"To the Amazon? Hell, no. Why don't you just try meditating?" he asks.

"Time and space. It's a skill, Mike. The guys in the Himalayas don't have iPhones and a daily schedule broken into fifteen-minute slices. The shaman gets it done over a weekend. I don't know if it's the brew they use, the music, or their own skills, but everything I'm reading says they can catapult you through the veil."

"What veil?"

"Away from the senses, self, ego. Separateness. The veil that conceals reality. The ceremony is supposed to shoot you over the fence, into mind. Deep consciousness. Ultimate reality. God."

"I have no idea what you're talking about, but it sounds like you do. Give it a try and let me know how it goes."

I don't actually know what I'm talking about. I've read about the shaman. The ceremonies. The plant brew they use. The connection to what some Hindus call the Third Eye; what the Ancient Egyptians might symbolize with the Eye of Horus. I'm more curious than certain.

"You see the stock market? Things are good, man, relax into it," he says.

"I'm not sure that's the leadership yardstick you want to be using... The fucking Tweets, Mike, you've seen them."

"He's authentic at least. You know what he's thinking, or not thinking, about."

"He farts with his mouth," I say.

Mike is laughing.

"He farts with his mouth and the whole world talks about it. Outrage. Can you believe he farted? A cloud of stink and thunderclaps of outrage... Every fucking day. The media loves this stuff but it's agitating, man. A daily thumbtack I step on reminding me something is wrong," I say.

"Let it go, man, there's nothing you can do. We're in Canada anyway."

"It's worse here. Everyone walking around preening that our leader doesn't pass gas. Infrastructure is falling apart, taxes are going up. The most promising businesses in the country right now are marijuana businesses. Weed, man. What's the plan for the kids? What's the world we're building for them? Grow up, get stoned, question your socially imposed gender, work for the government until the depression and anxiety kick in then go talk to a social worker?"

"It's not that bad and you know it," he says.

"It is for me. I'm thinking of leaving. Dubai. It's saner there. I can work, chill, and think about stuff without this constant irritation."

"Seriously?"

I don't know quite how serious I am. I've been talking to Mike about this for a few years. Never quite serious but never just joking either.

"Let's say I am. What do you think about Nancy and me moving to Dubai?"

"Without the kids?"

"Yeah."

"I think it's a great idea," he says.

There's no way Mike thinks this is a great idea. It's insane. I wanted to run it by him so he could talk me out of even mentioning it to Nancy.

"I spend so much time out that way, it's almost easier to just live there. Kids are getting older. They're always out. Emma is getting her own place. Amelia has already asked to go live with her. Jesse is going away to prep school for hockey, and Elliott has been spending more and more time with his dad."

"What does Nancy think?"

"We joked about it in the past. I'm not sure how serious I am. Just wanted to take your pulse on it."

"Why Dubai?"

"Not sure. There's something spiritual in that region, I think. Like a calling. A thing I have to do. You ever feel that? Like a thing you can't quite remember? I get that feeling sometimes with places. A weird kind of gravitational pull. I've felt it with London and I've felt it with Dubai."

"So, nothing to do with favourable income tax rates?"

"I think it'd be cool for the kids to use it as a launching pad to see other parts of the world."

"This has nothing to do with the kids," he says.

"Nancy really wants a fresh start in her career."

"Nope. It's not about Nancy either."

"Fine. It's sunny, central for me and work, and I'll pay less tax."

"That's better."

"Eat some carbs, Mike, the diet is making you grumpy."

"Honestly, I think it's a great idea. There's something you're trying to figure out. You've had this since I've known you. I don't understand it but I've always admired it. You've got a gap coming up now with the kids before there's any sign of grandkids, and if you don't do it now you never will," he says.

I'm waiting for the sucker punch. Mike usually opposes any idea I have on the general grounds that it's me having an idea.

"You're serious. You don't think this is ridiculous?"

"You're married now. Talk to Nancy. She's smarter than both of us and grounded. If it's right, you guys will figure it out."

"I take it back, Mike. This Keto deal, it suits you."

#

I call Fadi.

"Buddy! How's the green card going?" I exclaim.

Fadi didn't stay in Dubai very long before getting the itch and moving again. Just over a year in the desert before deciding to move to the US. There was a job offer he couldn't refuse, and it came with a green card and a choice of living anywhere in the country he wanted. He chose Maui.

Or I should say, he and his wife chose Maui. Fadi got married.

I spoke to him last summer. He had just met someone and it was getting serious. When we spoke again in the fall he told me he was getting engaged.

Jesus, Fadi, you've only known her since the summer.

Actually, no, I broke up with the lady I was dating in the summer. This is someone new.

Fadi is buck wild, and so is love sometimes.

They met in the fall and he proposed over Christmas. On top of the volcano in Maui. They eloped and decided to move to Hawaii with dreams of a surfer family. Mr. and Mrs. Buccaneer.

"I'm not sure, I'm a little worried," he says.

Fadi is emigrating to the US at a time when the subject has become suddenly controversial. He has a Middle Eastern last name and a skin tone that suggests mixed racial heritage. Most places he travels to this isn't an issue, but on the rare occasion in the US it's been a problem.

"You're working for a good company, they have good lawyers, they'll figure it out. How's Cath?" I ask.

"She's good. We're settling in. I think I'm going to donate my kidney."

"What?"

"Her kidneys don't work so great. She's been on a waiting list for a while. I'm not a match with her but there's a way that if I donate one of my kidneys, she'll be moved up the list."

Buccaneer with a heart of gold.

"Wow!" I exclaim.

"How about you?" he asks.

"I think Nancy and I might move to Dubai."

"No way! You sound like me now!"

"Maybe a little. It's not fully fleshed out. Might take us a year or two to work out all the details and logistics but I feel it, man, we're moving!"

"Congratulate Nancy for me. That's a bold move for you guys."

"Love you, brother."

CHAPTER 17 — A POPLAR AMIDST THE PINES

It's Sunday on the last weekend of summer. It's been over two years since the election. It took us two years of planning and preparing. A few occasions of cold feet—*Are we really doing this? Is this crazy?* We ran the idea backward and forward through friends and family, and most of all the kids. Some decisions look really smart or really dumb, but only after a little hindsight. I won't know about this one for a while.

I'm at the cottage. It's early morning. I'm sitting in the kitchen, looking out over the lake. The late summer fog is thick and the lake is still. Not a single ripple or wave; a perfect mirror to the cedar and pine trees along the shoreline.

It's a fitting morning. Quiet and ambiguous. The kids were supposed to be here last night but opted for a party instead.

Nancy is fast asleep. She was up most of the night doing a kind of reverse nesting. She's energetically preparing the cottage for our departure. I have a list of things to get through before we go. Most days I look at the list and procrastinate, but today feels like the day to start crossing some items off. Stock some firewood for the winter, prepare the backup water pump, bring in and store all my tools. I didn't get anywhere near as much work done this summer as I would have liked.

In our little corner of the lake, the pines and cedars have grown tall. Most of them are over a century old, more than halfway through their lives. Towering above them is a single young poplar that shot up through the dense underbrush to reach the sunlight. Its canopy is still full and lush but will soon begin to change colours; reds and yellows before shedding its leaves.

There is an ambiguity about this day, this moment, this period in my life and the times. Dread and optimism in equal measure of what is beyond the pines and the fog. Mike says I worry too much and he's probably right, but the equation in the back of my mind that feeds an underlying anxiety: there hasn't been a time in recorded history where so much power has been concentrated in so few people with so little wisdom.

Optimism isn't happy ignorance. It's about making a decision to focus on the best possible outcome. I'm optimistic, but that view isn't supported by the calculus my rational mind makes when I think about the leadership around the world. The complexity and scale of the problems on the horizon is the numerator; our ability as a people to unite, to communicate effectively, achieve rapid workable consensus and move on to the next problem is the denominator. Without expanding our common denominator, the math isn't pretty.

I think about the kids. The despair I feel about the world they are entering and the confusion about leaving them behind for a while. I don't know what being a good dad means anymore. I just know that it can't include pretending that everything is okay.

Jesse and Emma took the news of me leaving well enough. Amelia not so much. She didn't say anything the night I told her. Or the next morning. Or the one after that. She stopped talking to me. Finally, I chided, pleaded for her to talk. That I had been a good dad and now I needed her trust. The benefit of the doubt. That somehow, someway this was all going to work out.

"I'm not quiet because I don't trust you, I'm quiet because I'm fucking sad!"

Her words still ring in my ears. We haven't said our final goodbye yet. I hate goodbyes. I can't even say goodbye to TV characters on a show that I like; I've never watched the final episode of a series. And now I'm preparing to say goodbye to all that matters most to me.

#

Mike and Anne arrive at the cottage. They brought pie. Nancy's been cooking the vegetables and I've been working meat on the barbecue. We're having an early Thanksgiving meal together before Nancy and

I leave next month.

We sit around the old oak table I kept from my grandad's cottage. Anne sits beside Mike. Just like Mike, she's strong, funny, gregarious, and caring. They've been married for over twenty years and still laugh at each other's jokes and hold hands under the table.

"When do you think you guys will come visit us?" Nancy asks.

"We talked about it. We're thinking next fall," says Anne.

"We could stay in Dubai for a few days then all take a trip together and visit Egypt," Mike adds.

Mike knows I want to visit the pyramids. We've been talking about them a lot these last few years.

"Did you guys hear about the new comet impact theory?" I say.

Anne and Nancy look at me strangely.

"Alex doesn't believe the pyramids were built by slaves. He's into conspiracy theories," Mike says.

I'm not into anything, I'm just curious about the world and open-minded. I've also been around enough engineers and scientists not to worship at the altar of the status quo anymore. It wasn't so long ago the scientific status quo held that the earth was flat. In the same year Einstein won the Nobel prize in physics, surgeons were removing teeth and non-vital organs as a treatment for patients in insane asylums.

"It's not a conspiracy theory. I just don't think our current state of knowledge on the pyramids is accurate. We know the Sphinx has weathering patterns on it that are at least tens of thousands of years. And there are plenty of other clues that are counternarrative. I'm not saying that there's a better theory on the pyramids, just that the current one is deeply flawed, that we'd be better off teaching kids that the pyramids are an open question and a greater mystery than what we teach them now."

Mike is about to start debating before Anne cuts him off.

"Egypt sounds great!" she says.

"If we go, I also really want to scuba dive in the Red Sea," Nancy says.

Mike and I nod and smile. Marital instructions transmitted and received. We get up from the table and start clearing the dishes. I wash and he dries.

"Mike, you never let me finish," I say.

"That's because nobody wants to hear your crazy theories."

"It's not a theory… more like a wondering."

"About what?"

"That, maybe, there was a time before this one when we all got along a lot better, that we had a way of living and working that made sense, that religion helped propel people to greater heights of mutual understanding and creativity… there's a breadcrumb trail of evidence that makes me think it's possible."

Mike smiles and nods.

"Fine, Mike. You want to talk about the price of tires and who might win the cup next year?"

Mike laughs.

"I booked that shaman retreat," I tell him.

"Really, for when?"

"On my way to Dubai. I have to stop over in the UK for work and there's a weekend retreat in London not far from the airport."

"I thought you said the Amazon?"

"Urban Shaman. They have them in a few cities."

"Nancy going with you?"

"Nah, she's going to fly direct to Dubai. I think this is more of a solo deal, and honestly, I think a lot of this for her is happy talk. She indulges me but that's about it."

"I'm kind of curious. I looked into it after you told me. I'm not sure if it's for me, but I'm interested in what your take will be," he says.

"Yeah, we'll see. It's a little far away from hockey arenas and dogshit bags, but the timing is perfect, so we'll see."

"Speaking of, how did it go with Theo?"

"The kids were fine. We had a good weekend with him before saying goodbye. I talked to a few people and they told me adoption wasn't going to be a problem. For reasons that aren't clear to me, beagles are still very popular."

"Can't believe you lasted as long as you did," he says.

I had bonded with Theo but we never seemed to fully embrace one another. The relationship always felt a little one-sided. As long as there was food, he was happy.

"Almost six years, Mike. And not a single day I didn't regret making the decision to take him in. The best part, when we took him to the adoption place, I said my goodbyes and made my peace. I walk him inside. Amelia stays in the car. She's crying. I go to give him a hug and this dog just walks away without looking back because he smelled food."

Mike is laughing.

"Look at your kids, man. They're happy. They're engaged with life. They're independent and have dreams of their own. They went through a pretty tough phase and came out with flying colours. That dog had something to do with it," he says.

"It's funny, I dreamt about him the other night. Running through the forest trail. That's what he loved the most. Just following his nose. When I could get him out of the city off-leash, he was transformed and he became this other thing, like an intrinsic cog in this incredibly complex machine. He was a part of nature and I got to watch the show. It was beautiful."

"I'm going to miss you, brother."

Me too, brother. You have no idea.

Over the years we've spoken almost daily, but we've only really seen each other every month or two. But that contact, the lunches, the chats. That security of knowing that in any kind of emergency Mike would be there for me, that sense of fraternity and shared responsibility. It's a hole in my heart I'm already starting to feel.

CHAPTER 18 — PACKING

I moved my mom out to an apartment of her own last year. It's a nice, European-style, basement apartment. She's been happy. Got to know a few neighbours. I try and swing by once a month but with my departure coming up, I check in a little more often.

It's sunny and warm outside her apartment today. When she gets in the car, she immediately bursts into tears.

"I promised myself I wasn't going to cry," she says.

"It's okay, Mom," I say.

"This will be our last coffee," she says.

"I'm not leaving for a few more weeks. We'll see each other again." I'm lying. I don't want to deal with a goodbye today. I switch to pleasantries and avoid the weight of the moment.

She's gentle today. Over the years she's been loving, kind, and wise.

She's also been angry and distant. She has in her a tremendous curiosity and love for the innocence of this world, and at times a searing kind of hatred for everyone in it. She's been abandoned, hurt, disappointed by just about everyone she's ever dared to love—her parents, my dad, my brother and me, her grandkids, in-laws, friends. Her bruised heart throbs painfully with scars on top of scars.

My earliest memories are of her reading to me, poems from Khalil Gibran. She would carry me to the garden; the still, warm summer air heavy with the rich smell of life, soil, and tomatoes, alive with the sounds of crickets and sparrows. She gardened while I played by her side. She tended to my wounds, my scrapes and bruises. She healed me with her love. She tamed me with her wisdom. She taught me how to channel my anger as a youth, directing me toward understanding, compassion, and purposeful action. All life's challenges were lessons, all pain was growth. And then she broke.

The light in her dimmed. Her garden was overrun. The poems and life lessons had been replaced with pill bottles and simmering rage. She had become weary of life. She had stopped loving the world. Her love for me was diffuse, a distant lighthouse in a tempestuous storm.

The bond between us is sore. Each visit seems to bring with it a kind of pain.

We make small talk. "Look at my wrinkles," she says as she shows me her arm with pride. "Each one has been earned."

I smile and swallow back that lump of emotion building up inside me. I don't want this to be the last time I see her.

I drive her to the store and we slowly walk inside. She wheezes if we move too fast. She is holding my arm.

"I need to pick up a zipper and some yarn," she says after catching her breath. "The zipper is to mend my robe and the yarn is to finish the dress I'm making for my great-granddaughter. I don't think I will be around long enough to meet her, but I want to leave something of me behind. I'll make pants too, in case a boy comes along."

I start biting the inside of my cheek. We both know that great-grandkids are probably quite a few years away, but she's getting ready.

Neither of us knows if this is the last coffee because of my move or because she won't be alive when I come back, but she is ready. I am not.

#

Jesse just got his driver's license. First try. I pick him up in front of his mom's house.

We're going to drive over to pick up my dad and bring him to lunch. I thought Jesse was going to drive but he's not comfortable on the highway. At least with me beside him. On the drive over we talk about his upcoming school year. His hockey season. The makeup of his team. His ambition and maybe some of mine.

"What do you think about the burning rainforests in Brazil?" he asks me.

I'm a little surprised by the question. Jesse doesn't talk much and when he does, it's never about world affairs.

"I don't know, what do you think, bud?"

"Seems like a big problem. We need that forest," he answers.

Parts of the Brazilian Amazon are on fire. People argue about climate change. The voices are loud. I don't want my kids screaming into the wind. I don't want them thinking the world is full of heroes and villains. I don't want them picking imaginary abstract sides of multifaceted complex problems. But sometimes the problem isn't nuanced and the solution is painfully obvious: *Put the fucking fire out, man.*

"Bolsonaro's a donkey," I say.

The Brazilian president is refusing to accept financial help from the EU after French President Emmanuel Macron scolded him; the Brazilian tweeted that the Frenchman's wife was not as young and pretty as his own.

"What do you think is going to happen?" he asks.

"I don't know, Buds. You put a donkey in charge of a lemonade stand, you get a lot of manure and no lemonade. There are a lot of donkeys running a lot of lemonade stands right now, and I don't have a clue how this is all going to play out, but yeah, we need that forest."

#

I park in front of my dad's nursing home so it's easier for him to walk to the car. Jesse and I take the elevator to his floor in the group home. His door is the one with the hand-size bronze crucifix on it. Jesse knocks gently and we walk in. "Hey!" My dad is delighted to see us both, but especially Jesse. He's clean-shaven, dressed to go out, and couldn't be happier.

I do my level best to love my dad where he's at. I bury the frustration and resentment I have towards him deep inside.

We drive to a nearby upscale Italian restaurant. "Do you have chicken wings?" my dad asks the waitress. He can't hide his disappointment when she says no, but he tries. Both he and Jesse order chicken parmigiana, which wasn't on the menu, but the kind lady waiting on us doesn't want to say no twice.

"What's new and exciting?" my dad asks me. He then opens his mouth to hear better. His hearing is going with the years and he's too proud to wear a hearing aid. I don't know when the mouth thing started, but I know the more he strains to hear, the wider his mouth opens. If the ambient noise is really loud or the person speaking is quiet, he looks like he just saw a ghost.

I give him the lay of the land. The highlight reel of the last few weeks. He and Jesse talk about the upcoming school year. But mostly I try and sit quietly and soak in the moment. There's something special about being at a table with my father and son. There is a deep affection between the two. A love that is pure and unsullied by day-to-day grievances and petty moments. I like being around that. Seeing how they look at each other. It's spontaneous and genuine.

"How's your mom doing?" he asks me.

"She's good, Pop. She's good," I say, trying to deflect the conversation because I know what's coming.

"Did she ask about me?" he asks. Always with a flicker of hope that one day I will answer the question differently.

"No, Pop. No, she didn't," I say like I always do. It doesn't bother him like it used to, but it still bothers him. On his better days, he would move heaven and earth if he could for her. They loved each other in the way that two survivors of a shipwreck on a deserted island would, needing each other for survival but needing to be on separate parts of the island for every moment between. There were of course tender moments, a lifetime's worth. The trips to the hospitals, the dinners, the laughter, and the tears. He could make her laugh in a way that nobody else could.

Since I split them up, my parents barely have had contact with each other. The boy in me hopes that one day, somehow, they will find each other again without the rage, fear, and pain. That just one more time they will hold each other's hand and say *I love you.*

"I dreamt about her last night. I dreamt that she had passed away, that the police were looking everywhere for her next of kin, that I wouldn't have the money to pay for—" my dad says before I cut him off.

"Pop, you don't have to worry anymore. Mom is doing okay, and when the day comes that she isn't, it'll be taken care of. You don't need to worry. It's all going to be okay," I say.

He turns to Jesse, closes his mouth, and sees him as though for the first time. "What a beautiful boy," he says and cuts into the breaded chicken.

CHAPTER 19 — IRISH BLESSING

I've had a lump in my throat again for the past couple of hours. I said goodbye to the girls last week and was able to keep it together. I kept it light. Emma and Amelia would be the first to visit us in Dubai, and I focused on that. The girls draw on my strength more, a desire to be stronger than I actually am. More in control than I actually feel. With them I was stoic on the outside and a complete mess on the inside. Second and third guessing the decision to move. *What the fuck are you doing, bro?*

With Jesse it's a little harder. He's already his own man. He has an inner strength all his own. He sees through my charades. If the girls do too, they are graceful and polite about it.

I've been biting the inside of my cheek all morning, during a monthly management meeting which I spent most of on autopilot, listening and talking over numbers and spreadsheets, fighting back the impulse to run into my office and cry. Just prior to starting the meeting I exchanged a few texts with Jesse. We decided on driving to his college tonight. I'll be dropping him off tomorrow morning.

I pick Jesse up at his mom's home. She helped him pack; I help him load. She's quiet, her emotion near the surface. We exchange a knowing look, a gentle acknowledgment of an important milestone. Jesse stands tall beside her and they hug; she squeezes him tight and he squeezes her right back. I swallow another lump and chew on the inside of my cheek, sharp stinging pain to stay the tears.

We drive to my place, where Nancy has prepared us dinner, our last meal together. We eat and they say goodbye. Hugs and waves.

We set out on the evening drive. Mostly we're quiet. I desperately fight the urge to tell him one more thing, to try and guide and steer him. The seeds of wisdom are inside him. They will germinate and blossom in their own time, I know this, but I still fight the urge to say something. We stop for gas and water. He fills up, I get us the water. We drive into the night, the soft glow of the instruments on the dash and the lights of the cars we pass along the highway.

We talk about future careers, and most of his thoughts on the matter relate to making money. How much and how quickly. He wants to get out of school as quickly as possible to try his hand at real estate. "Jesse, don't worry about money. You'll make money no matter what you do," I tell him.

There's a useful little saying I've heard that you could divide your working life into three parts: learn as much as you can, earn as much you can, give as much you can. "Don't look at what you can earn, focus on what you can do, the problems around you that you can help solve, what you can bring to the world. The people around you will inspire you. Make as many friends as you can, be a good friend to them, and things will work out," I say, having finally failed to resist the guiding impulse. None of these things needed to be said, but there is one vital thing I want him to know. It's a fundamental worldview that shapes decisions and contributes to misery or happiness in equal measure.

Focusing on what you can get from the world is okay, but it's a relatively short and fruitless path. Moments of pleasure, distraction, and comfort are about the sum total of anything you can take in. Focusing instead on what you can give out is where the real party is at. What you can learn, become, achieve; the people you can help, the problems you can solve, the moments of harmony and love you can experience, and most of all, the people you can know intimately and share the journey with—that's the party. The moments of pleasure, distraction, and comfort come for free with that package anyway, but they are the interludes, the salt you sprinkle on the food, not the main meal.

"I know you like real estate for the money, Bud, but try and keep your mind open and watch for the thing that inspires you most," I tell him.

Mostly, though, I'm able to avoid the philosophy lectures and moralizing and we just share the space. We find a motel along the way. He eats again. We watch a little TV. We sleep.

The morning comes. I wake up before him and I listen to him sleep, the same way I did all those years ago. I watch him breathe gently. Peacefully. I watch him intently, squeezing the last bit of juice out of this trip, until he wakes up, heads straight for the shower, and off we go on the final leg.

We arrive at the college. The campus is electrified with youthful exuberance and potential. The excitement of young minds and bodies preparing for adventure. We move in slow motion through the registration lines, course selection, nursing checks, and the moment of anticipation builds. *I have to say goodbye to this child.* We drop off his bags in his dorm room and we set out to drop off the hockey bag at the arena. I steel myself.

I take a final picture in front of the arena and wrap my arms around him. I kiss him on the cheek and tell him how proud I am. I can't say anything else because the tears are there. I squeeze tight.

"I love you," I say.

"I love you, too," he says, and we let go.

I move to the car quickly and watch him enter the arena. Through the tears, I say goodbye. My child. I whisper the old Irish blessing.

May the road rise up to meet you
May the wind always be at your back
May the sun shine warm on your face
The rains fall soft upon your fields

And until we meet again
May God hold you in the palm of his hand

Godspeed, son.

CHAPTER 20 — TAKING OFF

It's cheat night tonight. A break from the keto diet we've been on again for the past few weeks. The house is sold. We've moved out. Nancy and I are having dinner in a nearby village to celebrate. A few more days before I go to London and Nancy heads to Dubai.

She's wearing a sweater with a big heart on it. She spent the day working outside with her dad, and she radiates the earth and is lighting up the room. The place we chose is an eclectic restaurant we like, always a good mix of older and younger crowds. And the best mussels and fries in town.

It's been a stressful period for Nancy. Lots of change for someone who is, at her core, an incredibly stable and grounded person; we are opposites in that respect. Too much stability and repetition and I start to die inside. It's in the balance that we find harmony and adventure. But the scales have been heavily tilted my way for the last few years, and now it's time for a period of stability. Our plan is to be away for three years. Three years without a change of address or profession. Three years of eating well, living healthily, and being attentive to each other. I can do that.

Mike likes to say, "When you make plans, God chuckles," and there's certainly a grain of truth to that. The threat of war looms larger today than at any time in the past decade. In the Middle East where we are going but also in the South China Sea where I spend a lot of time.

Our parents are approaching a time at which their needs might become pressing; our children are stable right now but still vulnerable to pressures that would alter our plans and trajectory. But all that being said, we do have a plan, and I'm deeply committed to providing as much stability as I can muster. So, we are starting with the basics: eating a healthy meal, together.

Three weeks into the keto, we're both starting to feel good about ourselves in a way that we haven't since we met. We've been in a five-year loving motion-blurred swirl of kids, renovations, travel, and work. Each day broken into fifteen-minute slices, rolling into the next. No more big changes after this. I get the value of stability. The importance of grounding yourself in routine. When the basic cornerstones of living are approached with a certain kind of discipline, a rich feeling of satisfaction emerges to underpin everything else.

We needed a break from the diet, but also from all the micro-decisions and transactions that come with a big move. Joint decisions from two smart, independent people with completely different perspectives and life experiences. We needed a break from the fear and anxiety that has continued building as we approach the big day.

We talk, we eat, and eventually I start sharing my passion, my enthusiasm about the shamanic ceremony and what I might learn.

"It's good we're on the keto. That's pretty much what the organizers are recommending we eat beforehand, minus the meat," I tell Nancy.

"You need to diet before the ceremony?" she asks.

"It's a part of the cleansing process, I think. Apparently, the weekend can be quite physically intense, and the fewer toxins in your body, the better."

I leave out the part about getting violently sick.

"They say you need to have some intention before you go. Something I want out of the experience," I say.

"What do you want out of the experience?"

"Honestly? I'm not super clear on that."

For some reason, I'm shy with her whenever it comes to my own inner search for truth and wisdom. I dance around words like *God* and *religion* because they are loaded words these days. For a lot of people, God is a brand. A symbol. If I say to some of my religious friends that I want to connect with God, there's a feeling of unearned loyalty, like we support the same football team. If I say the same thing to my atheist friends, it's a conversation killer, it's a warning signal to a rational mind that I might have a rigid set of beliefs and that I might be dangerous.

"Some people think that the shaman can help you connect to the mind of God. I want to see if that's true," I say. "And on the off-chance it is true—and don't laugh—I want to know how the pyramids were really built."

I'm mostly kidding about the pyramids. I'm more interested in the idea that an ancient ritual has within it a kind of spiritual technology that the new world overlooked. That maybe the modern shamans have found a way to reconnect man with the deepest of truths. That we are in a race against time, for our species to wake up to our deepest nature and rebalance the world before we blow it up or burn it to the ground.

I keep talking. I tell her about all the possibilities. *Hacking God*. I'm excited.

She smiles. She's patient with me. Because she's a patient woman. But she looks at me with a vague frustration—the kind of look she'd give a dog she loves that won't stop barking. She is deeply grounded in being; she spent the day outside, cleaning up her property. I spent a good part of my day floating in abstract clouds of possibility. She is weary, whereas I'm energized.

But it's deeper than that. She has spent her life within the institutions of the twentieth century: family, school, university, engineering, large corporations, government. I've spent my life outside them: I dropped out of high school, started a business, and never looked back. I work with the institutions now. Observing them, understanding them and their inner workings, exploiting their failings for profit and gain. I've seen the astonishingly limited intellectual and emotional perspectives of people in power. The absolute pettiness and sheer carelessness involved in far too many major decisions.

I am, in most senses, a radical and a rebel. There is a part of me somewhere near my core that wouldn't mind seeing all the great institutions burn to the ground, freeing all the humans trapped inside the gears of the 'system.' I think that, maybe, that's been the great religious message throughout all time: freedom. The liberation of mind and heart from a mindless and heartless institutional culture. I'm passionate about that and talk excitedly.

"Maybe this is a recipe for a kind of plant technology. A way of connecting with each other. A universal language of consciousness, meanings beyond words and symbols. Like nature's gift. Something to help advance our intelligence, our evolution..."

But the way she is looking at me is sobering because she's uncomfortable. It's a respectful sort of *Holy shit, I didn't realize he was crazy* look, and in her case one tinged with doubt, as in *Holy shit, did I marry a crazy person?*

I've seen this look before. I used to see it all the time, early in my career. I would present radical change in the form of technology to people—institutional people—and with few exceptions, the ideas would arouse more antipathy than interest. It took me a while to understand that however innovative or noble the idea behind the change, the degree to which it was a radical departure from the status quo marked the degree to which it would be resisted by the people inside the systems.

With time I learned that the cornerstone of a great idea is less the vision itself than the way it's presented. Punching people in the face with radical change is counterproductive, however well-intentioned it may be. The bedrock of the great idea is how you create the space in which to bring people along with you. It's about the bridge you build between the old and the new that people can walk over, each at their own pace.

But amid the enthusiasm of new ideas, it's sometimes hard not to bark, and barking new ideas at people is not loving. If you're not dismissed entirely, you are at best seen as threatening. And I get Nancy's look: *Stop barking and join me in this moment.*

"How's your fish?" I ask her.

"Delicious. You want to taste?"

#

Mike is driving me to the airport.

"Oh no," I say.

"What's up?"

"I forgot my dad."

"Forgot what?"

"Forgot to say goodbye. I got everybody. The kids, my mom, Nancy's parents... And I forgot my dad."

"Did you *really* forget? Or you just didn't want to see him again?" Mike asks.

Mike knows how I feel about my dad. I've been working on that resentment for years. Never fully able to let go. I don't know if I truly forgot or there was something deeper going on. Either way, I'm feeling regret.

I think of my dad. He's probably watching the TV news, glued to the presidential impeachment drama. The ultimate made-for-TV drama. He'll be wearing jogging pants and a tank top. His hair will be combed neatly but slightly askew from a snooze. He'll be like he is on most days now, two parts content and one part sad.

We arrive at the airport. I'm travelling light. A few suits for my meetings during the week and some jogging pants for my weekend meeting God.

Mike steps out of the car and gives me a big hug.
"Going to miss you, partner. Give me a call after the ceremony. Stay safe," he says.

"Love you, brother," I say.

"Love you too, man," he replies.

CHAPTER 21 — BUNK BEDS

I landed in London a couple of hours ago and I feel supercharged, filled with energy and excitement. That's the effect this city has on me. I've spent time in almost every major capital in the world, and London is unique in the way it changes me.

It starts with the airport: London Heathrow. If not quite the busiest airport in the world, it is the most efficient in terms of using its relatively limited land resources and airspace capacity to deliver over 200,000 passengers per day, a flight every forty-five seconds from morning till night. Passengers from everywhere to everywhere. At any given moment all the nations of the world are represented in Heathrow's Immigration & Customs hall. Rich in colours, sounds, and smells.

I love England and the British. In my travels, I get to experience a lot of different cultures, interact with systems and corporations, observe and listen to people from every walk of life. I miss living here. People here seem to analyze and complain about everything that doesn't work right in their country. Few leaders of any kind can rise very high here before the public knocks them down. To the average citizen, every leader is some version of a moron. It seems to be the default position.

It's a reasonable position; holding out for a superhero leader to sort through the mess is not the path forward. Whatever the future holds, it's on us, regular folks with cell phones and internet access. Never in human history has the ordinary citizen been this empowered. It's no wonder every leader sounds like some version of a moron; most people have access to more up-to-date information than heads of state. The world moves too fast for intelligence briefings and memos. Ditto for science, religion, and any other discipline. Millennia of accumulated knowledge and real-time global data feeds literally at our fingertips.

#

One day to go before the ceremony.

I call Nancy. It's her last day with Elliot back home. He goes over to his dad's tonight and she leaves tomorrow, so this is her goodbye day and she is short of breath. She lives how she feels, and today her emotions are right near the surface. She's excited and apprehensive. More excited than apprehensive, but it's a big moment.

Nancy and Elliott are especially close. Co-conspirators in life. They have a long-term plan and Nancy's move is a part of that plan. It might not be obvious or disclosed, but it's there and I envy them that. The plan.

I'm in the back seat of an Uber, speeding down the motorway toward the South of England. One more day of business and a breakfast meeting tomorrow morning, then I'm off. Off to the retreat and whatever secrets it may hold.

I watch a few more videos to prepare me for the ceremony. A little more information, but not too much; I don't want to project anything onto the experience. My main concern is losing my connection to everyday reality. The stone-cut oats, steak, and mashed potatoes of everyday living. I like this reality. As much as I may float off into a dream world from time to time, I'm surrounded by people who are grounded in the here and now, and I love those people. They love me. The last thing my kids need is their dad coming away from the weekend with a bandanna and a sandwich board to preach about the apocalypse. The last thing Nancy needs is a husband who is more detached, less present. I still very much love what I do as a career, and Monday is an important day of negotiations. I need to be sharp and focused.

I hope that following the retreat I'll be at a minimum unchanged— but I also hope, more optimistically, to come away as a better version of myself. More present, compassionate, and attentive. A better leader, husband, father, friend, son.

Mostly, I feel profoundly grateful for the world and for being in it at exactly this moment. I feel a kind of indebtedness. I have been given so much. It's a debt that I want to spend the rest of my life repaying in any way I can. I hope I will come away with new wisdom and clarity about how best to do that.

On YouTube, I watch an old man speak about the role of the shaman. The man speaks softly, with a nervous energy and excitement of discovery in his voice. He is not a monk. He does not seek the 'be' in the centre of being; instead, he chooses to explore the outer fringes. An ethnobotanist and explorer, he is speaking into the camera about the nature of the shaman. He describes the shaman as a person outside culture and time. A person that straddles the outer finite world of gravity and entropy, and the infinite and eternal inner world. He explains how the shaman can navigate that space and bring others along with him.

The shaman I have chosen—Sophia— took me a few years of internet research to find. I can't pinpoint any specific reason why I chose her, except for feeling that pull I feel occasionally. A deep and subtle intuition of the right path to take.

She understands something I don't yet.

#

It's the day of the ceremony. I'm back at the airport. The retreat group, a handful of strangers from around the world, are going to meet here before heading out to the ceremony.

It's been a busy week in my corporate life, and I was on a call this morning where some harsh words were exchanged. Well, maybe not exchanged. The harsh words came from me and were received by the person on the other end of the line.

My mood has changed. There is an aggression and competition in me. I'm supposed to meet a few people flying in and I'm not excited by the prospect. In fact, I'm mildly irritated. I don't like meeting new people at the best of times. I put up with it in my work life because it's useful and sometimes enjoyable; with fellow travellers and craftsmen working one way or another on the same global system, conversation is usually easy. We often know one or two people in common. The sense of humour is shared, mostly. But meeting people from different parts of the world attracted to the same shamanic ceremony is an entirely different prospect. I'm immediately confronted with a baked-in sense of superiority. The feeling that I will probably be the sanest person at the retreat. The most successful, or the most grounded, the smartest or wealthiest, and on and on I go. It's a carryover from the workweek, a confidence and vanity that occasionally serves me in the world of power and domination, but right now it's not useful. And at another level it's just arrogance and fear. At my core I'm generally pretty timid. I dress that up in all kinds of ways to get through life, but I'm still one part timid boy, and that's the part that has been around the longest.

I'm holding off on sending the text to let the group know that I've arrived. Another thirty minutes. A bit more solitude to recharge the batteries. Nancy is in the air, on her way to the desert.

I take my watch off. It's a nice watch, a sign of status and power in the corporate world. I put it in my bag and take out the prayer beads I bought in Hong Kong instead. The Po-Lin Monastery, a giant buddha on top of a mountain overlooking the city. I twist the wooden beads around my wrist. I feel there is something almost holy about them. If my watch is an outward projection of power and status, the beads are exactly the opposite: a reminder of who and what I really am.

I finally send the text, and before long I'm sitting at a table with three strangers. I was the last to arrive. I had hoped to find a quick rapport with at least one, but each of them irritates me in a different way. One talks way too much, one mumbles and is barely audible, and one looks at his phone after asking me a question. I'm starting to regret signing up.

Then I notice one of the guys is wearing a watch that I've seen before and like. Superficial and trivial, but right now it's a lifeline. I relax a little. I get to know my fellow travellers a little better.

John, the one with the watch, is an insurance guy from the UK. He isn't sure why he's going to the retreat; he overheard a conversation between friends and it just seemed like something to do at this stage of his life. Stefano: Italian name but speaks with a posh English accent. His parents emigrated when he was born. He's youngish, late twenties, born and raised in the UK and works in Russia. He's going to the retreat because he's searching for something and can't put his finger on what. And then there is Duncan, who mumbles. A returning vet from Afghanistan, mid-twenties, rugged, handsome, and almost completely incomprehensible with the thickest of London accents.

We share a taxi to the retreat. It's cold and wet outside and my feeling of irritation is rumbling. We enter the house, where there are even more people. I'm shown upstairs to a room with bunk beds. Three bunk beds. *Are you fucking kidding me?* I was expecting this to be a mildly luxurious spa retreat with a trip around the cosmos mixed in—a high five to God, an attaboy from the old man, and off I go.

The lady who shows us the room says it's just for our bags. We won't be sleeping in the bunk beds; we'll all be staying in the same room downstairs, the ceremony room. The one with fifteen thin mattresses stuck way too close to each other, separated only by buckets for people to be sick in.

Jesus, bunk beds was the upgrade.

I move into the living room, which is now filled with even more excited and excitable people. My irritation is peaking now, but on the outside I remain congenial. I engage as minimally as possible. No follow-up questions beyond the *hi, hello, and yes, I'm happy to be here.*

It's time to prepare for the ceremony.

CHAPTER 22 — MOLASSES

Fifteen strangers from all parts of the world together in a candlelit room. Mats on the floor. Most people dressed in white. Except for Duncan, sandwiched between John and me; he wore jeans. Stefano was out of sight on the other side of the room. The rest were mostly strangers to me.

I had gotten to know Duncan a little better. We smoked together outside before the ceremony. I understood about half of what he said, and I think he understood about the same of what I said, which was enough for me to become his translator for the rest of the group.

Duncan was troubled. He had experienced the horrors of war, been wounded, several times near death. But far more importantly, as far as he was concerned, he was having girl problems. He and his girlfriend had a complicated relationship and it was at a low point.

Most people there seemed to have some sort of issue to deal with. One lady was living a personal challenge she didn't want to share. She was hoping for the clarity and courage to change. A guy from California had dealt with bouts of crippling depression until his first ceremony. His life changed, the depression was gone, and this would be his third ceremony, his life having become richer and fuller with each successive exploration. Another lady just wanted to *trip her balls off*, as she put it. And a few people were just lost, stuck, bored, frustrated, living lives disconnected from any discernible purpose.

Sophia was in the centre of the room. She wore a white dress, but more formal. She was young, elegant, and pretty. She had two assistants. On her left, a young Swedish woman, and on her right, a dark-haired woman with the tone and demeanor of an aboriginal medicine woman. Her skin was slightly darker, her eyes slightly narrower, and they sparkled. She wore a feather in her hair. Sophia the Shaman in the middle, flanked by the Caregiver and the Medicine Woman. They flowed together. They worked without rules, just a kind of harmony, a music reverberating between them that I couldn't hear.

Sophia's English was slightly broken, with some Northern European enunciation and phrases.

"Before we start, I want us all to introduce each other, but not in the way we are used to. I will set a timer and we will stand and move around. Each minute you will look into someone's eyes. You will not speak," she told us.

In any other setting and at any other moment, this would have bothered me in the extreme. I could imagine how it would go down during business meetings next week, if a bunch of men in suits decided to mill around the room staring into each other's eyes for a full minute. To my everyday self this was insane, and the resistance I felt about doing this exercise was intense. But I was all in at this point, and my stare down started with Duncan, the wounded warrior.

I think it was the first time either of us had stared directly into another man's eyes. Our initial reaction was to want to make a joke, to minimize the moment, to defy the intimacy. But after about ten seconds of silent awkwardness, the defiance melted away. His eyes were bluish green, quite beautiful and deep, I would have said, if not for the beard and thick eyebrows framing them. Time slowed down. I wasn't counting the seconds. I was glad to be in the presence of this companion. I felt an affinity toward him, a sense of fraternity, as though on some day, long ago, we had fought together, as though he had once done something important for me that I wanted to thank him for. A vague sense of indebtedness without remembering why.

The minute came and went and we started moving through the room. One by one, strangers stared deeply into one another's eyes. Person by person, defiance and anxiety melted away. It was no longer a room full of strangers; it was an intimate gathering of souls. It was a sacred space.

By the second or third person, the contact ended with a hug that was spontaneous and automatic. With most of the people in the room the contact was uneventful. There were no feelings other than a general appreciation of intimacy and sharing what had now become a holy rite in a sanctified place. But with the Medicine Woman there was something else—a recognition, a connection, a knowing smile. She was going to be integral to the ceremony, I didn't know how but I felt grateful to be in her presence.

The Medicine Woman, feather in her hair, began a ritual. She lit some kind of incense and anointed us with the smoke, one by one. I no longer felt any sense of anxiety or anticipation about the ceremony. Concern for any ill effects—purging, as they call it, or vomiting or diarrhea—none of it mattered. I felt a profound sense of stillness, peace, and well-being, neither hungry nor full, poised, ready for whatever unfolded.

Sophia spoke again.

"Before starting, we will drink a homemade brew from the Amazon together. It is a plant medicine. Direct from Mother Nature. I made it here from a recipe I learned in Peru. It is what the shamans there have been using as part of the ceremonies for a very long time. "After you drink, please go lie down. We will be silent together for thirty minutes. For some people the experience will begin. Some will see intensive visual images. Others may feel extremely strong emotions. If you have pain or trauma this may be what you experience, and we will be here to help you. You may not feel anything, but later, in the weeks and months that follow, you will have important realizations—a feeling of certain things you must do.

"We will only do a little bit of the medicine for the first time. It is possible it may not be enough, and if after thirty minutes you want a little more, we will drink a little more. But please know, it is better to ease in. Once the medicine is in you, it can only run its course, so it is better to go slowly because it is a process we cannot stop once we have started."

She was kneeling before fifteen empty glasses. She poured the thick purple medicine into the first glass and offered it to the young man from the Netherlands.

"The medicine is very bitter. If you have trouble with the taste, please take a grape. If you must take water, please only take a little," she said.

The young man drank and took a grape. There was a woman who drank next, an eye surgeon from the Middle East. Then John, then Stefano. Duncan, and finally me.

I drank in one swallow. The taste reminded me of the molasses my grandma used to cook with. The dark brown, bitter-sweet liquid that she would let me lick off the spoon after she was done mixing. I hadn't thought about her in years, and I smiled, remembering the sweet warmth of her nurturing. My grandmother and I never once had a meaningful or substantial conversation. We never spoke about life. She didn't teach me anything in terms of knowledge. She was just a presence in my life—a loving and nurturing presence. She healed the small wounds. Made abundant meals. She cared. She loved, and I loved her right back. She fed me brown sugar and candy for the simple joy of watching the delight in my eyes. She pinched my bum whenever I ran past. I adored her. She was the hub of the wheel of our family, the gravity well we orbited. It was the simplest and easiest loving relationship I had ever known, and the first bitter taste of this plant-spirit medicine flooded me with memory of her. In this sacred space her nurturing care and love was present with me. I smiled, and I didn't need a grape.

I lay on my mattress and watched as the rest of the group took their drinks. I closed my eyes, and nothing happened, for quite some time. I felt no notable anxiety or joy, no physical reaction, just silence. When I opened my eyes I looked at Duncan beside me. He seemed slightly agitated. We looked at each other with nervous amusement. *Wonder who'll be the first to shit their pants?*

I alternated between closing my eyes, scanning the room, and smiling at Duncan. Someone on the other side threw up, briefly, then silence again. The ophthalmologist a few mattresses away from me started to groan. From the other side of the room, I heard muffled crying. I was smiling.

The groans became louder and the ophthalmologist began to speak. "Take me out, I want this to stop," she said weakly. The Caregiver went to her and began massaging her. She groaned again. "No, please, I want this to stop."

Duncan looked at me. We made big eyes and smiled. The groaning continued and the Caregiver began playing a drum. The beat of the drum didn't mask the groaning but almost seemed to put it into a different context, making it a note in a chord, a harmonious prelude. I was still smiling.

I closed my eyes again and listened to the sounds. In my mind's eye I started to see colours. I thought about Nancy. She sees all kinds of colours that I can't. I don't imagine in colours and forms. I think in words, mostly. If I close my eyes, I mostly see black, or a faded-out image of whatever I was just looking at.

So seeing the colours was a bit of a *wow* moment. I was awestruck. *I wish Nancy could see this. I wish everyone I know could see this.* The beauty was staggering. Such intensity, such sheer vastness and plenitude. It didn't answer the question of creation, it overwhelmed the question. *How did I get here? Why am I here? What happens when we die?* All melted into a singular moment.

Ohhhhhhhh. My God. Never mind the questions.

It wasn't a reverie. I was fully conscious. I could open my eyes and I was in control of my body, but something was different—how freely I could shift my perspective, from the colours to the sounds to my body. As though I had suddenly learned how to dance in the ether of my existence. My conscious awareness was no longer stuck right behind my eyeballs, the way it always had been. I was free. I could shift my awareness. I could follow a rhythm I had never known existed, and I could move with extraordinary ease.

There was music playing but I could no longer distinguish the sound from the light. The line between the auditory and the visual blurred, my own awareness continued to shift freely between them, and suddenly I discovered a new perspective. A new place for my awareness to sit. I was no longer just a spectator to sound and light, I *was* sound, I *was* light. My consciousness was dancing and my body smiled. The intensity and the degree of freedom I had to watch, to listen, to feel or simply to be—*beauty*. I touched my face and there was wetness under my eyes, my body crying.

Beside me Duncan made a sound. He was afraid. He mumbled, "What the fuck is this?"

The ophthalmologist groaned louder. "Please make it stop, I want it to stop. Please no more."

I shifted my perspective back to my body. I rose and put my hand on Duncan's shoulder. He mumbled again. "This is fucking mental, mate. What the fuck is this?"

The Caregiver was with him now. "Shhhhh," she said gently. She massaged and soothed him. She looked at me. "It's okay. Follow your own process."

I looked around the room and it had changed. Stefano was now sitting cross-legged beside Sophia. He was smiling. John seemed quite peaceful, lying almost in a fetal position. The Medicine Woman was walking around the room and seemed to be spraying water over one of the people lying down. Someone was leaning over the small bucket beside her bed. It was a kind of chaos, but it had its own sort of harmony. I didn't sense danger. I felt love. My feeling was that Duncan would be okay, and so would everyone else. I didn't need to be there, in my body. I could go back to being something else. I turned my back to the room and closed my eyes. Once again, I faded into colour and sound. *Love manifesting beauty*.

I moved beyond beauty and saw form. It surprised me. It was not what I would have imagined. What I was seeing was precision. Flowing geometry. Fields and folds of precise patterns. Precision is the signature of intelligence and what I was seeing was so overwhelmingly precise and at an incomprehensible scale. I moved beyond awe. There wasn't a word for what I felt, only a deep urge to worship.

Duncan's yelp pulled me back. He was screaming now. "Call my girlfriend! Please ask her to come and get me. I don't want to die... Will I die? Is this normal? Is this fucking normal?"

The Caregiver was over him. He was panicking. Terrified. "Shhhh," she whispered again. It wasn't an admonishment. I felt her love for him. She cared about him. She was helping him heal. I sensed his fear of her. He didn't trust her.

I took the prayer beads wrapped around my wrist and placed them on his shoulder. I put my hand on his chest and whispered, "It's going to be okay, brother. Hold on to these for me."

The Caregiver again whispered back to me. "It's okay, follow your process."

Although my eyes were closed, I had a strong sense of spatial awareness. My consciousness had a location—there was a forward and a backward, an up, a down, and a side to side. But there was more dimensionality to my movement. A compass is flat: it has 360 degrees of movement along a single plane. With my eyes closed I was still at the centre of the compass, but it was no longer on a flat plane. There were many planes. I perceived an indescribable vastness of area that I could explore. But I didn't. I focused the movement of my awareness to forward and backward. Forward was my body, and backward was light and energy. I moved backward without turning, my awareness fixed on a point at which my body existed.

The further back I moved, the more precise geometry unfolded to my sight. All was in motion. Flowing, folding, and curling. I marvelled at the geometry of a flower becoming a bird. *It's all one thing, one energy, one process. An eternal orchestra of creation.*

The closer I got to whatever was behind me, the less important the orchestra became. I was becoming bored, no longer curious. I could feel all desires wane, all my cares and interests melting away. No secrets could matter here, because here there were no secrets, no mysteries or puzzles. I was on the verge of profound understanding. I was at the event horizon of omniscience. The source of creation.

At the edge of the source was an awesome light shining behind me, through me, an overwhelming sensation of incredible love and joy. And, with my back still turned, I started to laugh. I did not feel the need to turn around, because I suddenly got the joke. I stood there for a moment and laughed at the irony. In front of me, up ahead, our vast cosmos was just a tiny speck inside the tiniest ripple and fold of this stunning tapestry of design, everything in flowing geometric motion. Behind me was a loving light. The Eternal Source. And I was laughing.

I wasn't learning something new. There was no feeling of joy in newfound discovery. I was remembering something I had forgotten. I was awakening to my most fundamental nature. I was laughing at the irony of a life devoted to understanding the world. All this time spent simultaneously asking and answering my own questions. All along, one part of me trying to unravel a mystery that another part of me was creating. It was silly. There was no mystery; there never was, I had just chosen to forget.

The light was no longer behind me, nor was it in front of me. The feeling of curiosity that I had been a slave to since my first day of conscious memory had disappeared. The questions, *how did I get here, why am I here, who am I* all faded into the light. And the laughing stopped. There were no more questions. There were no more patterns. I was infinite in potential, and totally without desire. My desire to exist was extinguished. I was everything or I was nothing; it didn't matter, it was all the same.

Any urge to create, heal, help, invent, love, or discover had disappeared. I was complete. I was at rest. And for a moment there was no longer any "I." There was no more perspective. No more awareness. I existed in potential, a raindrop in a storm cloud. An as-yet-to-be-born wave in a calm sea. Potential. It wasn't bliss. It wasn't anything. I was at total rest. Absolute freedom—free from being—free from the burden of existence.

For a few minutes, or millennia, I was Home.

Then I had the visions.

At some point during *my process*, I had two distinct *visions*. I use this word to differentiate them from dreams, but I'm not a fan of the word. In my polite and simple world, people who speak of *visions* are the ones you smile at and steer well clear of.

But I know what a dream feels like, and these were something else. They were purposeful, precise, and overwhelming. I felt like a student in the presence of a great teacher. I was learning something important.

The visions were so intense, I felt my body sweating and crying. The Medicine Woman was spraying water on me. She was slowly bringing me back to the world.

After the visions ended, the process felt complete. Two lessons that I could not quite formulate into words. Just a feeling that I had learned exactly what I was supposed to and no more. One vision was of my parents and the other about Nancy.

I was more awake than not. Deep in my awareness. Once again, I felt the light behind me. I was moving away, back into creation. I had perspective again and I felt effort. The weight of things. The work of consciousness. I wasn't sure if I wanted to move forward or backward. Moving forward was so much work. Everything was effort and focus. I was leaving a state of bliss for a body that had a job, a family, and material attachments. Christ, the caffeine and the nicotine cravings! Anxieties and worries that felt so pedestrian from this vantage point.

Closer to the world now, I felt the aches and pains of living return to my mind. What had become trivial in the outer reaches became important again. I asked myself before re-entering if I wanted anything to change about the world. I had a sense that I could, given a bit more time, manipulate the source code—that I could manifest and change reality with the ease of thought. I thought of my children, our children, and feeling like I could change anything, I chose nothing. *Wake them not abruptly from their dream nor their nightmare:* words from the vision of Nancy.

But in the last moment before re-entering the folds, I hesitated. There was one thing. One miracle. One last act. I paused for a moment and directed my awareness to my mom and dad. The vision about my parents. I made a wish. That my parents could be healed, just enough to feel love for one another one last time. In the heart and mind of my awareness I blessed them.

But there was nothing left for me to do in this space. There were no more secrets that interested me because there was no secret worth knowing. Life is the telling of an infinite story, a story we all are writing. I smiled at the scientist asking and answering his own questions, like me, seeking understanding instead of appreciation, caught in a loop, blind to the beauty unfolding before him. I laughed at the irony of any of us seeking earthly immortality, desiring to be stuck in these weak bodies and this tiny cosmos with so little power. Caterpillars desperately refusing to become butterflies.

My perspective shifted fully into my body. I opened my eyes to the Medicine Woman, sitting patiently beside me with her hand on my shoulder. She looked at me with tenderness and a knowing smile. She had been waiting for this moment since we first looked at each other. Confident and patient that my awakening would eventually come and an appreciation for being there to witness it. I looked at the feather in her hair and touched her hand on my shoulder.

I felt joy in the room. Duncan was gone. The Caregiver noticed me looking for him and smiled. "He's okay, he's upstairs sleeping peacefully," she said. John, my new friend from England, the insurance broker, began throwing up into the bucket beside his bed and I smiled. I didn't get sick or feel any the worse for wear. I felt only peace.

The ophthalmologist seemed immensely happy. She looked at me, smiling. "I'm a healer!"

I had been the last to wake up. Everyone else was up, sitting on their mats or speaking quietly to each other about their experience. I was still a little groggy. In the centre of the room, Sophia was speaking. She held out a kind of stick that made noise when it was shaken and asked us to pass it around. Each person was to shake the stick and say a single word.

The first person to receive the stick said *gratitude* before passing it on. The stick shook again and John said *love*. Stefano smiled broadly and said *compassion*. Then the stick came to me. I was still groggy but completely conscious of the entire ceremony. I shook the stick and said *Nancy*.

It echoed in the room, and a few people threw me quizzical looks. Sophia asked me to repeat myself, so I said again, louder and with more clarity: *Nancy*. The name meant nothing to everyone in the room, but after the vision, meant everything to me.

There was music playing. Modern songs. "Yesterday" by the Beatles into "Imagine" by John Lennon. Most of the group was up and singing. Sophia moved into the kitchen and started preparing a feast.

Stefano walked toward me. He glowed. He seemed brighter than the candles. He wrapped his arms around me and held me. We both were laughing with tears in our eyes. It was genuine and pure. John came and put his arms around our shoulders. We looked at the space where Duncan had been and exchanged knowing looks. He would be okay—better than okay.

In the room I felt the divine awareness, in the music and in the voices that joined in chorus. The whiteness of our clothes, the smell of the food, the colours of art, and the flicker of candles in the dark. And I thought again of Nancy: how much I want to love her, more than anything I have ever felt. To care for her, to protect her, to give her anything she needs to create. To endow this world with her beauty. I want to be beside her and bask in the glow of our love. I want to walk the world with her and share in all the beauty of creation.

Sophia had warned us against talking to anyone for a little while after the ceremony, because it would take us time to integrate our newfound awareness into the everyday construction of our experience. I, naturally, ignored this sound advice and sent Nancy a text. It was the gobbledygook of unintegrated love and excitement, but it was pure. It was me sharing a newfound truth, barking like a happy dog. And like always she was patient, but she was hurting. From across a continent, I could feel it.

"All this time… it was you." No qualifiers or context. For me, the deepest of truths and for her, a random electronic chirp.

I called and she didn't answer. She wasn't ready to talk. She was hurting. My pursuit of truth had been overzealous. It had been no different in function than my pursuit of power, I had been blind to love yet again. The pursuit of divinity is still a pursuit; it still blinds the awareness to the love and beauty of the present.

She was alone. In a new country. She was anxious and afraid. Overwhelmed. She was nest-less, living out of a suitcase. And one more time, when we finally spoke, I heard in the timbre of her voice patience and love. That I had a chance to undo the folly and exuberance of my youth. That I could take my place beside her as a man, as her man.

And then I slept.

CHAPTER 23 — HEART OF LOVE

It's a couple of days after the ceremony. I'm in a hotel room by the airport. It's early morning and most of the city is still asleep. Outside is dark. I hear the occasional sound of a car whizzing by on a highway, but mostly it's quiet. I think briefly of my new friends, still at the retreat, who are right now finishing their second ceremony; tomorrow will be their third and last.

I didn't stay for the second and third days. Not because I didn't like being there, or because there was something wrong with the ceremony. Quite the opposite. Despite my initial resistance and irritation, it was one of the most memorable and important moments of my life, and I couldn't have picked a better group to share it with. Having known them for less than twenty-four hours, they are now people that I care about, that I look forward to seeing again.

It was hard to leave. I wanted to stay and just be around them, but it was important that I spend some time in solitude. I left because I felt like a process had been completed; the exam question was answered. Nothing more would be gained from a second ceremony.

I am changed, and I need some peace, some silence, to process that change. To decode the visions.

I'm something of an impulsive person. I like to act on my unconscious thoughts, because in many ways that feels closer to truth than processing that unconscious thought for some lengthy period before acting. I like to speak and write in the same way, at the edge of consciousness, at the height of emotion and feeling. The most honest version of the ceremony and experience would have been whatever I wrote down yesterday. Fresh, unfiltered, and untempered. The trouble I'm having is one of perspective: Which version of *me* would be writing these words? I want everything I write to be as true as possible, but I want it to be cohesive, too.

I grew up with a conceptualization of God as a powerful man. *The Father.* As a child this seemed strange to me. *What about Mom?* As a father now, the concept seems ever stranger to me; that for thousands of years, Western religious doctrine puts forward the ultimate source of creation as a kind of fatherly figure. My first vision of the ceremony challenged this concept and brought me closer to my own parents.

In the hotel room, I close my eyes and bring the visions to the forefront of my mind.

I remember the power of the moment, the visions feeling more real than the world. I remember my ethereal body stepping into a strange but familiar landscape. There was desert and a night sky. Dunes in the darkness and shimmering points of light from a swirling cosmos. Inside the vision, I intuitively knew where I was.

I was deep inside the heart of eternal love.

There was a campfire. Two figures stood in its warm glow. He was wearing a glistening white robe and a keffiyeh around his head. She was wearing a black madraga. A little behind them, a silhouette of a sleeping camel. They were my ancestors. But they were not old. Nor young. They didn't look like anyone I remembered; I just felt their love for me.

They were dancing together, slowly. I sensed they were setting in motion the rhythm of the universe. That they centred the great wheel of time. She was looking into his eyes and he hers. His left hand held her right, their hands clasped between their bodies.

In this vision, my senses converged. What I saw, felt, heard, and understood happened simultaneously.

I watched the couple. She closed her eyes and rested her head on his chest in complete trust. He closed his eyes, tilted his head slightly, and rested his temple gently on her forehead in absolute appreciation. They stopped moving and held each other. This was important. They wanted me to see this.

I felt the reverberation of their love. Beyond the demands of passion and desire, I felt eternal love. My body wept at the purity of that connection and was awed by that power. The power of nuclear fusion, for two to become one. The asymmetric harmony of the glass figurine.

From their love for each other, flowed their passion for the world. I sensed their compassion. For me, a singular wave in a universe-size ocean full of waves. Then I sensed them asking me to do something.

I suddenly felt a little resistance. They were urging me to do something I didn't want to do. I didn't want to give them *the box*.

Deep within the well of *me*, far below the waterline, at the bottom with the slop and the slurry, I keep a locked box of shitty moments. Harms done to others, feelings of hatred and hostility, fear and loathing and shame.

Open the box.

I was flooded with empathy.

All at once, I felt the other side of each crappy moment stored in my consciousness and a sharp sting of pain. Regret, that my own stream of time only flowed one way. Actions that can't be undone and sins of omission, moments of cruelty or apathy, hidden but not forgotten.

Give us the box.

I bowed my head in embarrassment. I handed over the box. I did not sense their judgement. I felt only their tenderness. The warmth of their loving embrace.

Let it go, child.

Without motion, words, or gesture, they guided me. Moments of my life played through my conscious awareness. Like Ebenezer Scrooge, I was experiencing visions within visions. With each, they were teaching me, deepening my love and understanding, inching me closer to Wisdom.

In concentric circles from the outer edges of my life, toward the core of the people closest to me, moments whizzed by. With each, a healing thought or an insight. The moments ended with the two people that brought me into the world.

I was reliving a moment from my past with my dad. *They were showing me something that I missed.* A memory was replaying, but I was seeing it differently. I watched a younger version of me sitting alone in my dad's apartment. There were pill bottles on the floor. Under the bed. On the kitchen counter.

The ambulance had taken him to the hospital. It was his neighbour who called me. My dad had overdosed. I was at the apartment to put some of his things together. To get a sense of his life. I hadn't made time to call or spend time with him. I remembered his loneliness. He missed my mom. His grandkids. It was a vicious circle, the pills. The lonelier he got, the more pills he took and the more he pushed people away.

I scanned the room for a few things that could make his hospital stay a little more comfortable. There was a cross on his bedside table, I grabbed it. A pair of slippers. Some fresh underwear. Toothbrush and paste. I put them all inside a suitcase.

Beside the suitcase was his old leather briefcase. The one he carried to and from work every day. It was locked with one of those rolling numbered codes. '1234.' I remember opening it, the old files and brochures. He was his era's version of a travelling salesman—Director of Business Development for an aerospace company.

The pill habit started just before he got laid off. He was in his mid-fifties. In his mind, his career was past its peak. He felt he would be worthless in the workforce. The end of glory. No more *attaboys* from the executives, no more stories of victory over the competition, and no more admiration from the young men rising up the organization.

He spoke to me about suicide a few times. *I judged him harshly*. I judged him from a place of ascendancy. Me, rising in the world of power, wealth, strength. And he falling. There were so many things I thought a man and a father should be. By so many measures, I judged him.

Then I remembered the man who rubbed my hair in the morning to wake me up and sang a song at night to put me to bed. *You are my sunshine*. Every night and morning of my childhood. Kindness, patience, warmth.

The man who was fiercely loyal to everyone around him and, on his better days, could light up a room. His flower bloomed intensely until the petals decayed and his stem bent toward the earth.

He had been running from something all his life. And somehow, amid all that fear, he raised me.

Pop, all these years... so much fear... what were you so afraid of?

He taught me how to work hard, to survive and thrive in a corporate jungle. When I worked a paper route, he found me a better job at McDonalds. When I worked at a restaurant, he found me a higher paying job at a bar. "My boy will outwork every one of your employees. Give him a try!" he would say.

When I arrived at the hospital, the nurse pointed me down the corridor. I walked to a room he was sharing. The second bed was empty, but I pulled the curtain anyway to give us a little privacy. He tried to get up when he saw me but struggled with the IV drip connected to his arm.

"It's okay, Pop. Stay down."

I leaned over and kissed his forehead and sat on the chair beside the bed. I grabbed his hand and he squeezed mine without letting go.

He stared at the ceiling and his eyes were moist. All his strength was in the grip he had on my hand.

"I'm sorry," he said.

"Pop, you have nothing to be sorry about. I'm the one who's sorry. I haven't called or stopped by in—"

He cut me off.

"I missed you, son," he said.

A nurse entered and pulled the curtain back. "Just checking in," she said.

"Look at my boy… He's beautiful," he said to her.

I exchanged a smile with the nurse before she headed out.

"Do you think I should start dating?" my dad asked with a weak smile.

"I think you might want to wait for a different profile pic, Pop," I said flatly.

"They call it companionship. That's what I want, companionship."

"I think you would make a great companion, Pop."

"How's your mom doing?"

"She's good. Pop, we need to talk about the future. You think it might be time for a different spot? Where there are people to take care of you if you fall again?"

"I can't afford it. I can't even afford where I'm at now. I don't know how I'm going to survive next month."

The word *survival* has a permanent audio imprint in my mind. Whenever I think of the word it's his voice that I hear. Until the layoff, he had only ever been without employment for a few weeks in almost a half century of work. Lying in the hospital bed, he had a government pension from two different countries, disability insurance payments, and a son who loves him to help with the gaps. There was nothing to fear.

Pop... all this time you've been running... what were you running from... what were you so afraid of?

His words still ringing in my ears. The strength of his grip on my hand...

He's so beautiful... I've heard it all my life. *Look at my boy, he's so beautiful.*

The song he sang me every morning and night. *You are my sunshine, my only sunshine... you make me happy... when skies are grey...*

Ahhh, Pop.

He was terrified.

I was his ward. He was my protector. He was terrified of failing me.

He was afraid of not being able to provide, protect, and care for his family. The fear slowly tore this man apart.

In the vision, I held his hand tight. *Let go, Pop. You did it. You raised me. Let me take care of you now. Don't be afraid anymore.*

My dad and the hospital room faded into memory, leaving me with a feeling that I had learned something important. I was being ushered toward a new moment. The couple in the desert were showing me a new moment but one I didn't remember. I saw my mom but barely recognized her. She was so young, she looked like Emma. She was singing to a baby coddled in her arms. It was a Sanskrit song, an old story about a queen singing to her newborn son. The baby started to cry right after the king named him.

"Why are you crying, you are pure...
the name you have acquired is not yours
The body is not you nor are you of it...
You are pure, conscious, and taintless"

Then scenes from her life flashed by. Raising me. The garden. The poems. The plastic seat on the back of her bike.

In the vision, I was seeing my mom without the attachment of a son. I saw her as a woman. I saw her in a street full of other women. Her hair was red and curly. Her arms were raised. She was protesting loudly but I could not hear the words. I felt only the passion. There was a trash can filled with makeup and undergarments. A hand-printed sign: *freedom.* I felt the fire of justice burning intensely in her; the call of freedom and the passion to break from the shackles of oppression.

I felt her inner conflict, between the softness of motherhood and the harshness of the world. The turmoil of loving a man who was a devoted protector and unwitting oppressor both.

This is the tension of Life.

The sun, the earth, and the moon pushing and pulling; bodies simultaneously yearning for freedom and longing for union. She liked chess and he liked checkers; he was enthralled by her complexity and she envied his simplicity. Utterly incompatible, totally asymmetric, and at moments, in absolute harmony.

The moments flashed by and I watched her comforting a young teary-eyed man. It was me during the divorce. Her boy with a broken heart. I felt her body wincing, her own heart throbbing with my pain.

And finally, through the window of her basement flat, I saw her in the present. She was knitting. Sitting in a soft chair by the faint glow of sunlight filtering through plants in front of the window. She held the needles close to her eyes. She fought through the pain in her joints with a resolute determination to infuse each stitch with love and hope for an unborn generation.

At once, I felt the power and constancy of her love. Through the distance and the seasons, the triumphs and tragedies—the unwavering, unqualified affection and absolute love of *me*. *Oh child.* Sweet child of mine. *Feel it now.* Look deep inside my heart and *feel it all right now.*

I remember the vision of my mom ending and my ethereal body being back in the desert by the fire.

The couple had stopped dancing. The woman in black reached into a satchel and pulled out a clump of soil. She held the mound in her hand and invited me to look closer. I saw a stem of green and a nascent flower still in its bud. The plant was growing before my eyes.

A seedling. An ordinary garden-variety stem of a flowering plant unknown to me. Two inches of stem sticking above the soil, and a gentle loop with a closed bud. A humble seedling, green and proud, desire and beauty both. The will to push through the ground to feel the light of day, and the beauty of a burgeoning flower. It was the seedling of life, *this earth*, more precious than all the gold in the world, more meaningful than the answer to any mystery.

She looked into my eyes and saw that I understood.

In the hotel room, there are tears streaming down my face. In remembering the visions, I feel intense and overwhelming love.

It's the middle of the night back home, too early to call my parents. I feel so close to them. So grateful. To them and to Sophia, and all the events leading up to the moment I first felt the pureness of my own love. There's an expression I heard once: *Unity of Being*. I didn't know what it meant when I first heard it, but I feel like I do now.

The shamanic visions helped clear away old feelings. Things I was holding on to that were keeping me from this *Unity of Being*. Keeping me from absolute love.

I think the order I experienced the visions was important. The first vision was easier to bring into my world of reason and rationality. To feel more love and compassion in my own life. To feel connected to divinity, to feel that a loving power exists beyond my familiar everyday world. Out past the nicotine and caffeine cravings, there is a desert campfire with a camel and an eternal couple slow dancing around it, gently urging me to love just a little bit more.

It's hard to invoke the word *God* without causing controversy, but the intensity of the love I felt from the couple around the fire burned away any and all doubts I might have had. Whoever or whatever they were or were not, felt Godlike to me. Obviously, I don't know if their dancing set in motion the rhythm of the cosmos, but it sure felt that way.

Which is why the order of the visions was so important. The first vision was prologue. It was about clearing away the past to prepare for the future. The second vision is much more difficult to internalize. Harder to articulate without sounding batshit crazy, and the implications are more far-reaching in my own life.

In the second vision, my perspective had shifted. I had become the man around the campfire.

CHAPTER 24 — HALOS

I meet Duncan at the airport before he heads back to his hometown and I head to Dubai. We hit an airport bar. It's busy and noisy. I strain to hear and comprehend my new friend.

Duncan is feeling better. He speaks nonstop for almost the entire thirty minutes we sit on barstools next to each other. A stream of consciousness about his love for his girlfriend, his confusion about their situation, and his desire to be loved by her. The young man has been literally torn apart by war, yet his greatest fear is rejection by the woman he loves.

"She's so fucking smart, mate. IQ of a hundred and forty-two, I reckon. She knows me inside out. She sees through me, but mate, I see through her too. I see how vulnerable she is. Mate, one time, she had to write an essay. She didn't want to. She worked her ass off for five fucking years to get that diploma and here she was, at the very end, too afraid to take the final step. Too afraid of failing. And I told her: No fucking way you're not writing that essay. I'm locking you in this room and I'm going to bring you a glass of wine every thirty minutes and you're going to write... one hundred words, five hundred words, doesn't matter, just keep writing and I'll keep bringing the wine. Every half hour and you'll get there, because you're so fucking smart and you worked so hard for this. And she did, mate, she wrote the greatest essay ever and she passed!"

He laughs.

"All those years she was at school I paid her rent. We weren't married but we were exclusive, you know? And we're both loyal people. Neither of us fucked around, but I paid her rent because I believed in her. She's so fucking smart. Mate, it was almost all my military pay I gave her every month. I shit you not, I ate baked beans every day. Every fucking day, beans, sometimes on toast. And then she breaks it off with me."

He takes a sip of his beer.

"Her boss treats her like shit. They don't value her. She's smarter than them and they don't like that so they treat her like shit. I know she's hurt by that. I know she's confused. I think maybe she's taking it out on me. I'm at a low point. I'm changing jobs and maybe once or twice I went out for a beer and lied about it, but I never fucked around, mate. I'm loyal like you can't believe, I'm loyal and I'm loyal to her even now. I could step out though, mate, you know that, right? You know how easy I could step out, it's served on a plate for me, all I have to do is eat it, but I don't, because I'm loyal, you know?"

He looks at me uncertainly, then looks away.

"You know what the hardest part of war is? Coming home. I knew what to do out there. I knew my purpose. I was scared as fuck, but mate, I knew what to do. I died three times. Three fucking times my heart stopped. It was black, mate. Fucking nothing... but I could handle it, you know? With her I don't know. I don't know what to do. I was hoping this fucking crazy shaman shit would clear that up for me, would show me a new purpose, bring us together, but Jesus Christ that shit was fucked up. It's alright now, I'm going to do it again, but not right away, maybe in a few months. But look at me talking. How's you? Alright?"

"I'm good, brother," I say. "Good to be here and see you smile."

"How's your lady, she alright?" he asks.

"She's good. I can't wait to be out there and be with her, but she's good."

"Oh, wait—before I go, I'll give you your beads back," he says and reaches to his wrist.

"No, no, that's what I wanted to tell you. Those beads mean a lot to me, and I want you to have them. I want to wish you well on your journey. I hope you'll keep in touch and let me know how things work out for you," I say.

We get up from the bar and hug. A big manly bear hug from two men who have known each other for a shade over twenty-four hours. We walk out of the bar and say our goodbyes.

John and Stefano also drop by the airport for a quick goodbye. I had wanted to see them both before they left, and they wanted to see me too. Two more ceremonies for each of them, and with both a little more clarity and wisdom. Stefano had discovered a new vision for his life. He wanted to help people in a way that he hadn't before. He wanted to devote himself to anyone and everyone who could use a hand, who needed a little bit of compassion.

John was deeply emotional. Bursting with love. He had seen visions of people who were once in his life, people he had cut off, people that he resented, and he had a new understanding of them—a new love that he had never felt before. He wanted to reach out and rekindle those relationships, to make peace and break bread with old foes.

There was a burning intensity in their eyes. They were carrying the sacred fire, lit from. Being in their presence was wonderful. I was enveloped in their loving halo.

We made loose plans to see each other again, to have adventures, to refresh and renew what we had gained over the weekend. Before parting we held on to each other like long-lost brothers.

#

On board an A380 to Dubai. So excited to see Nancy—to make our new home.

I'm so happy I bounce through the airport like a puppy. It's been a few days since the ceremony and each day seems to be even better than the day before. I want to talk to people. I want to reach out and connect with them in a way I've never felt before. And the folks from the weekend, the strangers who stared into my eyes, I want to see them again. It's a magnetic attraction, a closeness I haven't felt with anyone but my closest family and friends.

I thought this was going to be the end of something, but instead it feels more like a beginning. That might have been the biggest change since the ceremony: I went in feeling old, like I was in the last few acts, and I came out feeling fresh, vital—like I've barely begun an incredible adventure that will last far beyond this life.

There are other differences, too.

I started praying randomly. Without realizing it, I found myself falling to one knee, with my head bowed and my chest resting on my raised knee. As a child, I learned to pray on both knees, head alternating between the pew below and the heavens above. We whispered words from long ago. We chattered. We asked and supplicated. Wasn't long before I gave that up.

But yesterday, after packing up my things in the hotel, I was on a bent knee. It was an unconscious movement. I stayed in the position.

No chatter, I just marked the moment. I felt only my own strength, dignity, and momentary separation from my own sense of self. I was creating a place for beauty, for reverence; neither an act of defiance nor one of submission. It was an act of sacrament in an airport Hilton. A bow to beauty and a nod of gratitude, for this, here, now. I am of this ground, Earth.

I have enough time before takeoff to call Mike.

"How was it?" he asks.

"I'm still processing," I say.

"Were you sick?"

"No. Felt great actually."

"Did you meet God?"

And I hesitate. I'd need a different language to communicate the nuance and distill a newfound awareness into yes or no questions.

"All my questions were answered, Mike."

"You see how the pyramids were built?"

"Yes, I built the first one. The rest are low grade copies."

Mike laughs.

"Seriously, you think the ceremonies are legit? Should I do one?"

"Yes, and I don't know. I do think at a minimum maybe you might get a different sense of what death is and isn't, and I think there's a kind of liberation to be had in that. That's good. The rest, I'm not so sure, I'm still trying to put words around it."

I want to tell him about death. About life. I can't quite connect the new understanding into words. I can't materialize this incredible living architecture of life and love floating around my mind into language. Instead, I fumble around the scaffolding.

"How do you feel now?" Mike asks.

My hair stands on end in ecstasy, and everywhere I go I want to bow and kneel. The architecture and design of this world... I feel like high-fiving every person I meet!

"Different. Better, happy, and that there's this thing, this wisdom that is, sort of, there for me now but that I can't quite articulate. It's like there's a part of my mind that's unwrapping a Christmas present that another part wrapped. There's a learning moment to come, a transaction, and then I'll know. The shaman told us it might take a few months for everything to click into place."

Sophia was emphatic that it will take some time for the insights from the ceremony to fully materialize. Spiritual awakening is only the halfway point; integrating the divine wisdom and intelligence into everyday experience takes a little longer.

"Sounds a little crazy. You speak to Nancy yet?"

"Briefly yesterday. It's night over there now. I'll be there before she wakes up. We have to talk more about this, I'm just not sure how to put it all into words. I'll call you from Dubai, flight is taking off."

"Safe flight, brother," he says.

#

As soon as I landed, I rushed into a cab and drove the mostly empty streets through the early morning sunrise. I arrived at the hotel and raced to the elevator. I entered the room quietly and found Nancy fast asleep. She sleeps delicately, soundless, motionless, at complete peace. I prayed again, on one knee, this time a simple thank you, before taking my place next to her. I put my arm around her. She put her hand on my face, moved it through my beard, to my hair.

"I missed you," she said, sleepily.

"I love you," I said. Beside her again, I was home.

CHAPTER 25 — ARABIAN ORYX

It's late afternoon. The sun hasn't started to set yet. We are driving from Dubai to the Empty Quarter. Past the city of Abu Dhabi, with the Grand Mosque and the only Louvre outside of Paris. A couple of hours and the road takes us a few miles from the UAE's border with Saudi Arabia and Oman. The Empty Quarter. A desert the size of France. Sand dunes the height of tall buildings.

"So beautiful," Nancy says.

She is mesmerized. The road that takes us deeper into the desert is a thin strip of black on a vast canvas of brown sand and cloudless blue sky. We see a white Arabian oryx by a small shrub in the distance. I pull over and we get out of the truck.

Nancy is quiet. She's trying to zoom her phone camera to photograph this beautiful creature.

She's captivated by the oryx and I'm fascinated by the shrub. In the middle of a sea of sand, a lonely shrub. Planetary life emergent.

I'm transfixed.

I soak in the moment. Since the ceremony a few weeks ago, my ability to witness beauty and feel love has been multiplied. I've changed, or at least I'm changing. On the side of the road, in the middle of this desert, I'm struck again by the urge to fall to my knees.

In spiritual terms, language can be an encumbrance. It's a constraint to the imagination. But here in this desert, I feel it all at once. The sun heating the wind, the wind shaping the terrain, the evaporating dew in concentrated pools, a lush green isolated shrub, blazing white Arabian oryx out of view. Blue, green, white, red, sand, wind, water. Nancy shares a photo on her Instagram. Radio waves travelling instantly around the world, the light of the screen hitting her family's eyes and whatever sensation that evokes. It's all one thing, one process, one moment.

How the heck is falling to my knee with awe and reverence not the sanest thing I should be doing right now?

"It's so much nicer than in the pictures," she says.

I nod. I've been struck dumb.

We get back in the truck and start driving the last leg to the hotel. We decided to come here last minute. We booked yesterday afternoon. It's a celebration. Nancy found a job that she's excited about. We've moved into the apartment. We are settled and ready for 2020.

The hotel looks like what would happen if you sprinkled fairy dust on a desert hut. Thick clay walls, grand old wood archways, fountains and pools. It's a desert castle minus the spires. When I booked over the phone, I mentioned it was our anniversary. Upon arriving we are escorted to a couch in the lobby. A young man brings us cold towels, a silver plate of dates, and an ornate bowl of tahini.

"Oh my god," Nancy says as we enter our room.

"We're going to be okay here for a couple of days," I say, smiling.

The room backs onto the desert and the sun is setting behind the dunes. "Thank you," she says as she embraces me.

We stay up late and talk. I tread lightly around the ceremony. I don't mention the visions. I speak a little about the colours and the awe. If there is any use to these kinds of ceremonies, visions, or the spiritual life writ large, I need to show that through the actions I take. I feel like the world may already be full up on preachers and gurus.

Mostly we focus on Christmas coming up. Seeing the kids again back in Canada, what kind of meal she wants to prepare. Our plans for the new year. She tells me about her aspirations, for her career, for Elliott.

We talk until she falls asleep.

I head outside. Quietly I open the patio door and sit on the porch bench. Beyond the portico, hundreds of miles of sand dunes and black sky. The Empty Quarter night sky is a canvas for the stars to shimmer. I can make out the great river of stars that the Bedouins once navigated by. It is one of the spiral arms of the Milky Way. If I could sit here for long enough, I would see it swirl.

With Nancy asleep in the room behind me, and the stars shining above, I feel connected to the second vision from the ceremony. The one of Nancy and the pyramid. I want so badly to share it with her, but I can't quite find the conversational entry point to say, "Hey baby, do you remember that time we were Gods?"

There is no agreed-upon definition about what a mystical experience is or isn't. There are no rules about who gets to have them and who doesn't. Near as I can tell, every mystical experience ever recorded has two things in common.

The first is that the person having the experience is so overwhelmed by it that they absolutely need to share it with others; that they see people struggling and suffering and they want to touch them gently and say *it's okay – you are okay, this is all okay, it all works out, it really does!*

The second thing common to all the mystical experiences I've read about is that they are next to impossible to communicate in the rational space. In language. Which is a problem for me, because I can't sing, dance, or paint. Any of those things would make it easier for me to express to Nancy what I felt when I had the second vision.

I'm not a great conversationalist either, especially not in French.

In this vision, I was disembodied. There was no couple or desert campfire. I was floating in the ether. I felt tired and old.

I heard a voice. The voice was coming from somewhere beyond me, but it was my voice. It sounded weak.

"Nancy... Babydoll. Remind me again why we created the world?" the voice said.

The voice was feeble, and it repeated the question a few times. Like I was listening to a moment in time, replaying itself in my awareness.

Louder now. "Nancy... Babydoll. Remind me again why we created the world?"

"Aw, sweetie... you forgot again?" she said.

"I'm tired, baby, I feel like I'm getting old. Do you remember why we created the world?" I asked again, and she laughed.

"So we would have a cosmos for you to chase me in," she answered, laughing. Memories flooded into my awareness as her words rang out.

I remembered two points of light speeding away into the blackness. Separate straight lines. Then interwoven. Then joined as one. I saw a pyramid floating in the darkness, and flashes of design. I felt an attachment to the design of the pyramid. *That is my design.* "I built this for you," I said, surprised by my own statement. The great pyramid was my first gift to her.

"This is form and rule. Geometric precision. From this, all the rules of form in the cosmos can be derived. From this pyramid we will build the world, and from this you can reveal to it your beauty," my voice echoed.

From light, she gave us form. In the centre of the pyramid, we stood naked before each other, her hair flowing to her shoulders, and in her eyes, I could still see our light. Her features were so delicate, the curves of her hips, her breasts. Her skin glowed in its softness. I traced the line from her feet through the inside of her knees and thigh and I felt desire for the first time. I looked at my hands, my feet; I felt my face, the stubble of my beard...

"Why am I so hairy?" I asked and she laughed again.

I held her in my arms and we become one. I *felt* love for the first time. I loved her. She loved me. In the centre of the pyramid, we loved. In the centre of the Great Pyramid, I sired the cosmos and she gave birth to the world. She held Earth in her arms. I held her in my arms. Out of the pyramid flowed the river that fed the oceans. Beneath its stones grew the land and from its peak came the sun and the stars.

From her heart she grew the world and filled it with her beauty. She created the bees and the flowers, the swallows and the branches for them to perch. The fish and the fowl and the algae and grasses for them to feed. The delicate balance, competition and cooperation so finely tuned, unbegrudgingly favouring our welfare. From so few rules, so much beauty. She created.

"It was you! It was always you! Every spring, in the blossom of the cherry tree, the song of the melting ice in the stream, the first chirp of the waking bird, it was you!"

Other points of light came and through her they were born into the world. From me had come the design rules. The hard edges and patterns of existence. The angles and properties of structure, the geometry in which our world could take shape. From her came beauty, the manifestation of form. I was desire, she was beauty, together we loved. And through her the lights came and took their manifold forms: her children.

And then we forgot. It was the price of admission to enter the world. We fell into our own creation and forgot our origins. I had lost her, and thus began my chase. I leapt from star to star, searching for her.

And then I felt the sharp sting of pain hitting my awareness.

"Baby..." I said meekly.

"Baby... I fought wars to be with you."

In my youth I lusted for her. I sought dominion over her beauty. I warred for her. Endless battles of rage and blood. I created the warhorse and gave it strength. I could make it leap like a locust and strike terror with its proud snorting as it reared and stamped and charged into the fray. It was I who drove children to die on battlefield after battlefield. I who blasted the trumpets and I who stepped over the dead and the dying, always searching for her.

I swelled her river with torrents of the blood of her children. I fouled her sacred waves with gore. I searched for her in the stars, in the forests and deserts, across the oceans and deep beneath the seas. And then I sought to conquer her creation; that if I could not find her, I might create her. Thinking that if my power were great enough, I could bend her to my will. Imprison her and never lose her again. I scorched the earth she had endowed with her beauty.

In this remembrance, the shame, the folly, the suffering and pain I had caused...

"I couldn't see your beauty anymore. I only felt my desire. My lust for you. Our children tormented and suffering for my foolishness. I set fire to your creation, hoping to find you in the embers. I poisoned the air so you might fall out of the sky. I dried out your oceans and tore the mountains asunder, always in vain. Blinded by the vanity of my own power, my glory... and baby, you never stopped me. You just kept spinning your beautiful weave. From the torn lands of my battlefields you grew the poppies... in the scorched earth of my deserts you made the cactus grow. Our children, you loved them all. Baby, I'm so sorry."

I felt her hand on my head. Her delicate fingers moving through my hair. I reached my hand to hers and held her finger. "I don't want to chase you anymore, baby. I don't want to forget you again. No more wars, baby, no more battles or bloodshed... no glory, just you. I just want to be beside you, to watch you restore our creation, to lighten the hearts of our children."

She moved her head to mine and I felt her love for me. Her hand moved across my face. Through my beard and around my neck. Over my chest and stomach. Behind the small of my back. She pulled my body close to hers and whispered to me. "We need to forget one more time, sweetie. But this time you will remember that you are not a warrior... that you are a guardian. A protector of truth. You will tend to my garden with gentleness and care. War for me no longer, and dance. You will dance around the fire and beneath the stars. You will write for me. You will love me with your words. Your buildings, your creations will not be for glory, but instead they will be testament to our love—bonfires for our children to dance in the glow of our love. You will light beacons so that my lost ones can find their way back to me. Wake them not abruptly from their dream nor their nightmare but point to the light that will guide the way back home."

The vision ended with those words.

Something in me is changing. A strong sense that there is a shift happening in me and the world. That maybe we've been living in the era of the warrior king and a paternal conceptualization of

God since Alexander the Great and that maybe we are heading toward a more balanced time.

I think of the world I grew up in. *God the Father.* I think of my brothers-in-arms. The warriors. The conquerors. The soldiers and generals. The authorities, leaders, executives, and careerists. The fathers. The brothers. The league of manhood whose quest for dominion over the world would soon end. They will laugh and rejoice with me in time. Glory will cede its place to Beauty; the conquistadors will fall to their knees before that which cannot be conquered or ruled. They will fall to their knees and weep before the beauty of this world, and they, like me, will feel the shame of their folly and rejoice at true power, the love and awe they feel inside their own hearts.

\#

I wake Nancy up early. It's still dark out. I hadn't slept but I wasn't tired, and we booked a sunrise yoga session.

"Is it morning?" she asks.

"Almost," I say.

We head out early for the session. The instructor, a young man, guides us to the top of a dune. He brings two mats for us. I've tried yoga before and didn't like it. I want to try again, but not today. I'm not quite ready. I wave my hand to say that I'm going to keep on walking. There is a higher dune I want to climb.

The sand is cool on my bare feet. I reach the peak and look west. Dunes and shadows as far as my eyes can see. I turn eastward. First light. Pink rays. A hundred or so feet below me, Nancy in a yoga pose facing the sunrise. Her back is to me. She is standing, arched, arms reaching toward the sky.

On the top of the dune, I kneel on one knee and bow my head. *Thank you.*

Part III – The Yogi

And then it was the old woman who simply said: Hear me now.

CHAPTER 26 — THE GREAT RAKE OF 2020

Dubai, UAE, Summer 2020

I walked out of the Shaman Ceremony in late 2019, full of energy, vitality. Eyes toward the heavens, a blissful stroll, a profound sense of peace, love, and goodwill. Then I stepped on a rake labelled 2020.

You been quiet, you okay, bro? I send Fadi a text.

So angry... tried to stay away from the phone all weekend. I'm putting Noah to bed and I'll call you, he texts back.

Fadi and Cath had a baby, then back-to-back kidney transplants. Him to a donor list and her from a donor list. Their son Noah is all of two years old now and he's all that Fadi talks about. Almost.

Noah's bedtime in Maui is lunchtime here in Dubai. Nancy and I are doing a hybrid vegetable and fish diet. I have a little routine where I open the fridge door, look at all the vegetables, then look down at the floor, close the fridge door, empty-handed, aimless, and maybe a little sad. I do that a few times before making another coffee, and Fadi calls.

"Hey" he says.

His voice is deflated. I haven't heard him like this since his divorce.

"What's going on?" I ask.

"I'm just a little worn down. Cath is sick—food poisoning. Noah was down a little bit. And the fucking knee, man."

Fadi almost never swears.

Last week a man died on camera. Images went around the world. The man was handcuffed, lying flat on his stomach beside a police car. The man was surrounded by four police officers. One of them was kneeling on his neck. The man could not breathe. He begged for air. He begged for his life. He died. The officer kept his knee on the man's neck minutes after he was dead. Just before he was killed, the man cried out for his mother. His mother had passed away years earlier.

The police had been called to the scene by a deli store owner. The dead man was accused of using a fake $20 bill. He was trying to buy cigarettes. The man had two daughters.

This is important: the melanin levels of the men's skin differed. There was a fraction of a fraction of difference in their ancestral DNA.

"I know..." I say softly.

"It just doesn't make any fucking sense!" he says.

I stay silent.

"It feels like we're so fucking lost, man," he says. "That football player. He kneeled during the anthem. Such a strong guy and such a gentle move. He was vilified for just calling attention to this shit, man. The kids, man, they have to be taught how to be pulled over, how not to get killed by the law. It's fucking insane."

"I know."

I don't, actually. I've never worked as a policeman and I've never been afraid of the police. I've travelled around the world and never felt any less than welcome wherever I landed. I don't worry about my children the way some parents have to worry about theirs. I don't have to teach them anything about interacting with the police. They don't need to worry. And because they don't, I don't. I've lived a life of comfortable ignorance.

If I'm following the monk descending the mountain of transcendence, I want to turn around and go back up. There are more ethical challenges for me than when I started. The plight of the black community in America is harrowing. The state of the Western body politic is perplexing. The drums of war are beating a slow but rising rhythm in the South China Sea, and in other flash points around the world. Old ones in the Middle East and new ones along the Indian–Chinese border.

Closer to home, my business has been eviscerated by the global aviation shutdown. We had our first and only layoff in two decades since I started the company. The pandemic was a wave that washed away wealth and livelihood. Everything is happening so fast that I can barely process, let alone feel or think about anything. Feels like 2020 has lasted several years and we're only halfway through.

It started off innocent enough: a trip to Hong Kong and a hike up the Path of Wisdom in January. Now it's only June and I feel like Noah minus the apocalyptic prophesy; just a strange urge to build an ark. And I wonder what his wife was thinking. Was Noah's wife cool with the guy building a boat on dry land and talking out loud to random animals, or did she smile painfully and gracefully accept that her husband had lost his mind?

CHAPTER 27 — CONFUCIUS

January 2020

I'm on a flight to Hong Kong. Short business trip to meet up with a business acquaintance and celebrate a deal. The trip also gives me a chance to pick up a new suit and head up to the Po-Lin Monastery to replace the beads I gave to Duncan.

Nancy has been checking in a little more than usual. There have been significant protests in the streets of Hong Kong and rumors of a new virus. I'm a little worried about her. The US and Iran have had some tense exchanges not too far from where we are living now. Stressful times.

I've had a few nightmares. This is new. Other than the occasional remnants of a faded-out dream, I generally wake up with nothing but coffee on my mind. But since the ceremony, I've had a few. The nightmares are so vivid. Like the shaman ceremony, so intense in colour and feeling.

The first was of Emma. It was an anxious and helpless vision—she had returned to her ex-boyfriend, as bad an idea as she could possibly have. I could feel that her love for him was such that her path would be filled with pain and disappointment. The heart wants what the heart wants. I was powerless.

The second dream was about Jesse. He was playing hockey and he got hurt. More fear. He was motionless on the ice. I jumped over and ran to him, but again I was powerless.

The dreams leave an imprint on me that my conscious mind toys with for days after. Are they prophecies? Should I take any action? My occasional run-ins with wisdom feel like a safe being unlocked. A part of my mind is spinning tumblers until there is a distinct click and the safe opens.

After these dreams, it took a few days before I could access the vault and see the dreams for what they were: my frailty returning.

During the ceremony, and for days after, I had a sense of infinite potential—omniscience, omnipotence, invulnerability, and fearlessness. But none of that can serve me here. This is the realm of frailty, fear, and the fragility of life. My greatest vulnerability is the health and well-being of my two eldest children. I worry for them in a way that I don't worry about Amelia, who is a force of nature. With her I worry mostly about the application of force, the people that can be helped or hurt by her journey—but with Jesse and Emma I worry about the delicate nature of their existence.

The dreams grounded me. I have a base level of anxiety. I want to keep my atoms and cell together, my heart beating and, all things being equal, a full head of hair. The worries that seemed so pedestrian during the ceremony became monumentally important again. I'd like my kids to thrive, and it'd be nice if the world could avoid a nuclear holocaust.

For the rest of the flight, my mind toys with the deeper insights from my experience that haven't fully materialized into conscious space. Something about the feminine—a feeling, an intuition that I don't quite understand yet. During the ceremony I had heard the word *Gaia* repeatedly. I didn't know if this had been external, part of the music, or something internal. I still don't. I've asked a few people from the ceremony, but nobody seems to remember or know.

I'm starting to reconnect to *me*. I know this because what I'm mostly looking forward to on this trip is the new suit. I try to rationalize that I need it for business, but I already have a closet full. I don't need it; I just want it. Hong Kong has some of the finest tailors in the world—trained at Savile Row, they say. Some of the best fabric and material from Italy. And horsehair for the canvassing. I had planned on just one, but the salesman, a young man from India, was first rate. The black sheep in his family, he informed me, because he had married outside his culture—an Australian woman.

He knew all my buttons. He's dealt with men like me his whole life. He knew exactly what to say, and when. He was a pro. I bought three suits. Three shirts. Two ties. I salvaged a tiny bit of dignity by refusing a second pair of pants for each suit.

"Are you sure? It might be the last of this roll of material. There may be the slightest variation in the next roll, and I want your pants always to match. You will wear them out faster than the jackets," he advised.

#

I am walking through the narrow city streets, smiling after meeting my new friend. A good sales guy is always appreciated. If you leave a place having spent money on a thing, and you feel grateful, lucky that you got a good deal, that you feel well informed, that the thing you got is special, different, unique, you probably just met a good salesman or woman.

There are no protests today, but the evidence is still there. Graffiti. Broken signs. Leftovers from the mayhem.

"Beneath this mask
There is an idea
And ideas are bulletproof."
The graffiti is accompanied by a V for Vendetta logo spray-painted on a building.

There is tension in this city that I didn't feel before, but the Buddha doesn't seem perturbed. High above the streets, sitting in a flower on top of a mountain that overlooks the bay, the giant statue of the Buddha is equanimous. I head over on the cable car one more time.

Leaving the cable car, I follow the crowd and walk through the courtyard and gardens toward the stairs that lead to the statue. I see a dog, sleeping. And then another one. It's not quite noon and in the middle of a crowded courtyard on top of a mountain beneath a giant Buddha on the other side of the world, there are sleeping dogs all around me. Cognitive dissonance, something not quite right about the visual field. Throngs of tourists. Shops. Eateries, a Starbucks, and sleeping dogs.

I've been here a few times, and the sleeping dogs always bring me into the present moment. I feel oddly connected to this place.

Walking past one of the dogs, I bow my head slightly and smile. Like falling on one knee after the ceremony, my body just kind of does things now before my conscious mind can catch up. *Bro, what was that all about?* My inner dialogue has also changed. It's mostly gone but for the occasional quip.

I stop in the trinket shop and buy some new beads. Sandalwood. I twist them around my wrist. For Nancy, I pick out a glass lotus flower. The petals around the base are similar to the petals upon which the Buddha statue sits. I set out to climb the Path of Wisdom and the trail up to Lantau Peak.

It's my third attempt. The first time I had to rush to make a flight and I only got halfway up. Second time was with Nancy on our honeymoon. We were jetlagged and only got as far as the monastery. This time I'm determined to get to the top.

The day is overcast but warm, humid. I'm sweating. I seem to be alone. With all the protests, Hong Kong has few tourists these days. I climb for close to an hour up the stone stairs and gravel path. When I finally reach the summit, I take a selfie and send it to Nancy. I'm proud. I feel a sense of accomplishment, that I had finally completed a journey. After seven years, I've summited.

I am on top of a small part of the world. At once, I see the outline of this island and the sea. I rest one knee on the ground and bow my head.

Lantau Peak is a few hundred feet above the Buddha and maybe a mile away. I look down at the statue, small from my vantage point but his raised hand looks like it's waving at me. I wave back. *I made it.* I take out the crystal lotus flower and lay it on a rock to watch the colours dance from the refracted daylight. I stare at the flower and look at the faraway Buddha. The light strikes me in just the right way.

Insight, the lotus flower. The glass ball in the middle, with the light refracting. The petals. It's the source. That place outside time. Unity of Being, home, the place of oneness—the same centre of light and love I experienced during the shamanic ceremony. Transcendence.

I want to high-five the Buddha. From the peak, I wave peace and bow my head.

Now what do I do?

There's an old story about a monk who is trying to scale the mountain of enlightenment. Along the way he passes another monk, carrying a backpack, on his way down. The ascending monk asks in wonder, "Did you get to the top? What was it like?"

The descending monk throws off his backpack and raises his arms to the heavens, wordlessly. The ascending monk then asks, "And now? What is it like now?" The descending monk picks up his backpack and slings it across his shoulder.

Awakening is only the halfway point.

#

I meet up with Kwok, a business acquaintance, for dinner. We've met a few times over the years on my travels through Hong Kong. He's an engineer, businessman, and a grandfather. Our conversations usually revolve around family and global politics. Last time we met he promised to tell me more about Confucius.

It's been a few years since we last met. He has aged, obviously, but more than years. The night should have been a celebration of our recent business win, a contract in mainland China, but Kwok isn't feeling it. He seems a little despondent.

We avoid politics this time. He is reluctant to speak about the protests. Instead, we speak mostly about family.

At one point Kwok raises his hand gently and says, "I grew up in

Shanghai and before, once every month at least, we took the train back from the city to the village where we were born. We stayed with our families. Today, no more. The kids are busy. The kids play games. The kids know everything. The kids do not spend time with their family."

His world is changing too.

We don't know each other well enough for Kwok to have shared what he's really feeling and why he is downbeat. It's easy enough for me to project my own unease about the state of nations right now. He's only a generation removed from the wars of the twentieth century. He would have experienced the aftermath and first-hand accounts of the horrors that I've only read about. He would have been a young man during Mao's cultural revolution. The purges and the famine. He was a young father during Tiananmen Square. I wondered if as a grandfather he thinks differently than as a father. If Kwok, maybe, senses threats to peace and stability in a way a young father doesn't.

I had hoped the night would be a celebration and a learning moment for me. A lesson on Confucius. Some optimistic insight on the demonstrations in the city. On the growing tension between China and the West. Mostly we just eat in silence.

When I finally bring up Confucius, he says, almost dismissively,

"To Confucius, women were nothing."

#

Back at the hotel, I'm reflecting on our conversation, because his words triggered a thought. I flick through my phone looking for pictures of my honeymoon. For pictures of Angkor Wat.

The incredible layout of the temple and grounds in perfect harmony with the sunrise and the land around it. The astonishing laser-cut precision of the stonework—every square inch of the vast temple covered in stone wallpaper of arcane symbols and illustrations. Great stories told along the walls near the entrance. And then I find the picture I was looking for: Nancy, standing in front of a goddess in the centre of the temple's most hallowed precinct.

The goddess is sculpted into the stone wall, foremost among all the stunning works I saw in that temple. I took multiple photos of it; I was fascinated by its beauty. A woman stands with regal attitude, her right hand delicately placed over her womb, her left arm bent and its slightly upraised hand holding the stem of a plant; on her head is a kind of crown. She is wearing a symbol of the temple as a headdress, and rising from the temple, the patterns of geometry that span the walls of the entire temple; her eyes are closed. Her look is one of peace. She is dreaming.

She is dreaming the world. Gaia is dreaming our world.

My entire life, the books I read, about wisdom, ancient scriptures, Marcus Aurelius, Plato, Jesus, and Buddha—always men. My experience with Sophia the Shaman, the ceremony, my grandma and Angkor Wat, I finally encountered the feminine aspect of divinity, of wisdom. Everything I learned until now was only ever going to be, at best, half of a story.

And thinking about that connects me with the feeling I had after the shamanic ceremony.

The word that echoed in my mind: harmony.

It started with my grandma. With the realization that she had been the centre of the family; that my grandfather hadn't kept our family together so much as he had served her, on bended knee—cared for her, loved her. In the final years of their marriage, he would tenderly put drops into her eyes, several times a day, so that she could continue to see. And she let him love her, and together they loved, and it was this that kept order in our universe. It was their unity that kept us together. Masculine and feminine energies in harmony. The dance of yin and yang creating the balance that pulled us together.

I think back to that night watching the election with Nancy.

In the 2016 US presidential election, the final two candidates were a man and a woman. It was, however, a masculine competition in form, intended for a male-centred model of authority and dominance. As systems go, it is unbalanced. The Greeks extolled the virtues of their democracy and waxed philosophical about its greatness. Nations throughout our time have adopted in one form or another, in whole or in part, Greek democratic systems. But these systems were designed, root and stem, for and by men. A democracy born out of male-centred religion. Warrior-kings. Fathers and sons. Authorities and subjects. Masculine science. The hard edges of dominion over nature, tearing away her veils, slicing her open to dissect her being, under the cold lights of fact and reason.

I don't know what a balanced system would look like. But I do know that asymmetry and equilibrium between masculine and feminine are cosmic principles. And creating harmony today isn't about forcing symmetry or statistical representations of sexual organs on corporate boards or democratic institutions, but rather the reimagining and evolution of these systems. It is the wholesale revolution of our culture toward the balance of the best in man and the best in woman. It is in balance that we find unity, that we dance, that we love. And the gods cheer. This is not utopia; it is our natural state of being.

The first atomic element in the periodic table is hydrogen. A single proton and electron. Positive and negative. Yin and yang. It is that harmonious relationship that is at the very centre of life. In the twentieth century, we discovered a way of breaking that centre apart. Turns out that if you attack the core of life with a subatomic hammer at just the right angle and velocity, you can unleash the wrath of the Gods upon the world. *Nuclear fission.* The crowning achievement of many generations of unbalanced societies.

It's the same lineage of culture and thought that invented the steel elephant trap. With razor-sharp teeth, it maims slowly as the creature writhes in agony.

That is the profanity of the three-legged elephant: the unbalanced society that would tolerate the very notion of their existence.

CHAPTER 28 — ONE-WINGED MOTH

Nancy and I are in our new apartment in Dubai. It's early morning. I'm sitting at the kitchen table with an empty coffee mug, staring at the decorative plate of fresh avocado and bananas in the centre of the table. Mostly, I'm just lost in thought. Nancy just woke up. I've been up for a few hours. She walks over to kiss me good morning.

"Are you okay?" she asks me.

Not really. I want to quit my job, run away to the Himalayas, and become a sadhu. I want to wash my face with the ashes of the dead and protest this fucked-up world. Something in me is changing and I have no idea what. Nancy is pulling me into a world I don't want to be in anymore.

"Yeah, I'm good. My chest is just a little sore and it's distracting me."

I might be having a heart attack. That makes me nervous, so I smoke and eat a little more.

Run as fast as you can, worry about where you are going once you get there.

This is my life now. I'm in the middle of a corporate race I have no desire to be in, let alone try to win. I feel disconnected from the religious community I grew up with. I feel a tightness in my chest that hasn't gone away since Hong Kong. I feel like a bird trapped inside a nuclear submarine. I can't change course because I am grounded in the virtues of my grandfather that are pushing me to keep going. *A man should be steadfast.* Finding inner peace and resolution in a cave full of monks is out of the question.

"Here, stand up," she says gently. I stand and she embraces me, holds me tight. She moves her hand across my chest and lingers over my heart.

Breathe.

I saw a doctor in my twenties. Told him I was having a heart attack. He smiled and asked me what was going on in my life. He listened patiently to my laundry list of fears and then told me to take a warm bath and stay in it as long as possible, focusing on my breath. "If that doesn't work," he said, "try yoga."

Eat, Breathe, do Yoga.

It's a sign I saw in Maui. I tried yoga a few times and despised it. There's the pain of stretching and the boredom, the general feeling of doing something pointless. Underneath those feelings though, is a slight irritation with the community. The very notion of yoga. That twisting myself into a pretzel is the strangest form of escaping the responsibilities of daily life. I can't imagine the men I respect and admire doing yoga. Churchill doing the downward dog. Neil Armstrong doing the shoulder stand.

Desperate times, desperate measures. My least worst option in reconciling what I experienced in the shaman ceremony and life right now: trying to see if my foot can reach behind my head.

"You want to go to yoga?" I ask her.

"But you hate yoga."

"That was before the shaman," I say, trying my best to smile.

#

We are walking over to the evening yoga class Nancy picked out for us. It's winter now here, which means the nights are cooler. Some of the locals, or those that have been here through the summer, wear jackets. I'm wearing yoga shorts and a yoga shirt that fit slightly too tight. I'm optimistic that they'll fit better over the coming weeks. Nancy is wearing brightly coloured yoga pants. A new colour. Somewhere between orange-pink and red.

We are strolling along the boardwalk. To our right is the incredible cityscape of Dubai. Jumeirah beach, apartments, hotels, restaurants, and children. Everywhere children, families, from all parts of the world. Playing, running, laughing, and parents intermingling, looking on. It's peaceful here, in a way that I've rarely experienced in nighttime walks in big cities.

We arrive at the tall steel-and-glass building where the yoga studio is located, on the thirty-third floor. Enough of an elevation change for our ears to pop on the elevator ride up. Enough of a vantage point to see Dubai Marina in its full nighttime splendour. Walkways, canals, boats old and new, dhows, and yachts.

The studio is more zen than sport. Cushions on the floor, intricate hanging string chairs, and a large bench carved out of a tree trunk.

We remove our sandals, lock up our phones and wallets in the small lockers. We enter the class and grab a mat. Nancy heads to the front. I head to the back. I place the mat as far away from anyone as I can. I'm a proud guy. This isn't going to be a glorifying moment for my ego. I'm surrounded by a dozen or so people. Mostly women but in front and on both my flanks are men. To my left, an Asian fella; in front of me a younger man, looks American; and to my right, a curly-haired Norwegian. I don't know if he's actually from Norway, but his skin tone is pasty white and his features are vaguely Nordic.

The instructor enters the class. Tall dark man, sleeveless shirt and a flamboyant yellow scarf. His stature belies his voice, slightly feminine, higher pitched than I was expecting.

We start easy enough. Sitting.

Oh shit.

Not even ten seconds in, I want to stop. Just sitting in the recommended way is painful. The instructor introduces himself to the class and I'm missing half of what he's saying. He says something about intention. What is my intention? *How about get me the hell out of here?* That good enough? Time is crawling. My ass is hurting. My spine is bent. Around me, everyone is smiling. *Savages.* Their posture is perfect. Their spines stacked neatly. Legs crossed nicely. Head tilted up ever-so perfectly. They are in unison. The room is a garden bed of neatly arranged flowers, moving to the rhythm of the breeze.

The man at the front speaks quickly and the flowers flow and change shapes. Like magic, their forms morph. Into small animals, rabbits and snakes, into majestic Greek sculptures, they move together. He speaks single words: *Chaturanga,* and the flowers spontaneously transform. *Mountain pose* and they bend, fold, arch, squeeze, and stretch. *They flow.* Their movements are synchronized. Somehow these transformations are linked in a way that is apparent to everyone in the room except me; I move like a one-winged moth. There is no flow for me, just a dizzying whirl of motion, effort, sweat, breathlessness, and humiliation.

But I'm not giving up. This is clearly not the beginner class I thought it would be. *Nancy is a saboteur.* I see the instructor looking at me. There is a look of pity in his eyes. He makes his way to the back of the room and discreetly helps me balance a pose. I want to tell him not to bother, that this is a hopeless case. *Triage.* Let this patient go and focus your energy on the ones that have a shot at surviving. But I can't speak. I'm at his mercy. I'm kneeling or in some version of a child's pose. He's stepping on my feet and doing something to my bent-over back. I think he's hurting me, but my pain sensors have been maxed out since the class started.

"You have the strength. Keep going," he tells me. Or I imagine it. I don't know if I'm hallucinating. I think there is music in the background or chanting. Nancy is moving effortlessly up ahead. I think I'm angry at her. This is a beginner class in the same way that a street fight with Mike Tyson is a beginner lesson in boxing. The mat below me is soaked.

There is little thinking going on. The odd thought whizzes by my conscious awareness. I look through the glass wall at one point, wondering if building security is coming to take me away. I keep trying. I don't stop. I'm setting the lowest possible bar, laying a foundation of mediocrity that my future self will gloat in surpassing.

I hear the instructor say something about final poses. Thank you, Shiva, Brahma, Lakshmi, or Vishnu, whatever Hindu God of mercy has helped end this.

I am lying on my back, in the totally appropriately named *corpse* pose, while everybody else effortlessly flips upside down onto their heads. The physics don't seem right. Pretty sure I'm hallucinating. The teacher mentions something about the menstrual cycle. That some of the women in the class should avoid the next few poses. Good enough for me. I don't have ovaries, but I may have internal bleeding.

I excuse myself from the next moves and stay in the corpse pose.

The class ends. The instructor seeks me out. He's bright and beaming. I'm happy also, deliriously so, like a freed hostage. I get to return home! He says some kind words to me. Compassionate words. Meant to encourage. I don't really hear them, but I'm grateful that he didn't make me leave the class or have me arrested.

Nancy opens the locker because I can't bend over. I convince her to take a taxi because I can't walk. We head back home, in silence because I can't talk. Nancy is happy. Excited. She is sharing her enthusiasm for the class, having found such an amazing yoga centre so close to home, but I can't really hear her.

My mind is still. I've been beaten into submission by a kind-hearted dark-skinned man with a yellow scarf.

And I have a plan. I'm going to hire an Indian fella that I saw in an ad, here in Dubai. He's a yoga specialist, but it's a different kind of yoga, one that can help actualize wisdom.

CHAPTER 29 — GAYATRI MANTRA

It's early morning at the condo. Nancy is at work at her new job. I'm waiting for a private lesson with the new yoga instructor. It's been a few weeks since the pain and humiliation of that first class. Enough time to recover from the trauma.

The condo isn't huge but has floor to ceiling glass and a view of the water. It feels bigger than it is. When Rajesh arrives, we need to move some furniture around before we can put the yoga mats down.

Rajesh is in his late twenties, bespectacled, small diamond earring in his left lobe, and the thinnest of moustaches. He's mild-mannered, slightly awkward, and from a place in India that I had never heard of. His wife and young daughter are still there. He's building his yoga business up here so he can bring them over.

I instantly begin to like him. The religious and spiritual teachers I gravitate toward have this look: brightness in the eyes and a curl in a lip. Like they have a little secret inside them that they are bursting to share with you, but they are wise enough to know that they can't. The secret makes them happy. The inside joke. The inevitability of truth; that one day you will know that same secret and you will smile too.

When we spoke over the phone, I was energetic. Full of all kinds of questions. I had asked him about religion in India. The sacred temples like Kailasa, an entire temple grounds carved into and out of stone. Like the Great Pyramid and Angkor Wat, buildings almost impossible to conceive of building today. About the sadhus, gurus, the mystics and the yogis. *Tell me, young yogi. How do I square my life with the world? How do I move forward into this storm of chaos toward goodness? Please tell me what to do because I don't know anymore. Please, good sir, show me the way home.* He responded flatly. "Do you have a yoga mat?"

He lays his mat down parallel with mine. "Lie down on your mat," he says. I follow his instructions and he starts to giggle.

"What's funny?" I ask.

"Your body. When you go to the mat. It makes a sound. Like a heavy boot dropping on the floor."

We're going to get along just fine.

I'm stretched out on a black rubber mat. Rajesh is sitting cross-legged in front of me. We start with some gentle movement, basic breathing.

We work through a few different poses.

"Or just try your best," Rajesh says.

He says that every time he overestimates my level of ability to perform an otherwise basic stretch. I feel like he might be a gifted teacher and perfect for me. When this Indian man speaks English there is a lilt. A cadence. A rhythm and inflection to the language not present when I speak it. His words have a musical quality that my mind begins to reverberate to.

He is singing and my body is tuning into his song. "In-hale" and my arms rise, my stomach expands. "Hehhxhale" and my body folds, chest over knees, hands floating above the mat. Vriksasana, tree pose. Balancing on one foot, the other foot tucked into my thigh, arms raised above the head. I like this pose. I feel competent in it. I can rest in it and enjoy my spine straightening, my foot strengthening.

I already feel a sense of connection with Rajesh. A kind of intimacy where I can just be. For a moment at least, the world just is, and I can just be. We sit cross-legged, facing each other. He begins humming "Ah-Uhm" and I join him. I keep humming and Rajesh chants gently, a hymn, a prayer in a language I don't understand.

The session ends. I mirror him. My hands together in prayer. "Chanti, Chanti, Chanti." *Peace, Peace, Peace.*

He smiles. I'm smiling also.

"Do you know the Gayatri Mantra?" I ask him.

"Of course," Rajesh answers, laughing.

I had just learned about it yesterday and thought I'd ask. I'm learning that the mantras are a vital part of spiritual practice. The importance of sound—specific sounds. How reverberation affects the state of mind, consciousness. It's probably obvious to any music lover, how certain music can change moods, inspire, generate energy. It's less obvious, at least to me, how these mantras can. But then consciousness is subtle and wisp-like, I'm beginning to learn.

"Before you pick your mantra, you need to find which is your God," Rajesh says. "For me, it took ten years. I studied the Gods and the practices until I found the one that most resonated with me."

There is a subtlety to the way he uses the word *God* and the way my people back home interpret it. For Rajesh, he is speaking of a God the way I might speak of a comic-book superhero. Growing up, all my friends had their favourite superhero. For different reasons, some liked Superman, whereas others gravitated toward Batman or Spiderman. Each hero represented a set of ethics. A way of interacting with the world that inspired a certain kind of devotion. This is what I think Rajesh is telling me. First you pick your hero, then you follow the practice and ritual to bring out those heroic attributes in you.

"Once I picked my God, then I find a Guru, a specialist in that God and he initiates me. From him, I learn the mantras and the practises to which I then devote myself," he tells me.

"If you want to do a lot of commerce, maybe you select Lakshmi, and you will focus on wealth and good fortune. If you want to study and learn a lot, you could choose Saraswati. For many people it's Krishna or Ganesh. We have so many."

"Who did you pick?" I ask.

"Shiva," he says, smiling.

Of course. I laugh. What are the odds? Of all the Hindu Gods, the only one I'm remotely familiar with is Shiva. I was travelling through Kuala Lumpur, Malaysia, and came across a giant gold statue of a Hindu God. It wasn't Shiva but his purported ancestor. It inspired a little bit of internet research and I became fascinated by Shiva. He is mostly depicted as a kind of peaceful warrior. Handsome, strong, sitting in the lotus position with his eyes closed and a cobra around his neck and a trident in his hand. A mystical badass.

"What made you pick Shiva?" I ask.

He's shy about this. He deflects a little. I persist. Rajesh switches the subject. He tells me about his wife and daughter. How he misses them. How he can't wait for his business to be strong enough so he can support them here, and finally he relents.

"Shiva is you know... an alpha," he says, and I smile at him. This young man wants to walk the world with the strength and confidence of a mystical warrior. *Attaboy.*

ALEXANDER THOMAS

I understand his reluctance to share more detail. The God a person picks is an intimacy. Maybe because it reveals the deepest of aspirations within them.

"If you love Krishna, it is very relaxed. You want to be peaceful, like Buddha. Loving. Easy living. I love Shiva. This is maybe not quite as peaceful. It is change. Transformation. Intense energy. He is the Adiyogi, the first of the yogis," he says, and I smile again. I like Rajesh.

#

Rajesh and I meet regularly, a few times per week.

After a few sessions, I noticed that I've become randomly happy. Like by accident. I just notice occasionally how light my mood is. How slow my thinking is. That my ambition and restlessness have receded. That I don't really want to do anything other than just hang around and connect with people I love. I smile easier and I chuckle a little. There's a spring in my step and love in my heart.

On the mat, I am lying down on my back.

"Today I will play for you a mantra, a Shiva mantra," Rajesh says.

He touches his phone and the wireless speaker begins to play. There is a uniquely beautiful quality to the deep reverberations of a man humming from his depth. If a flute effuses its delicate melody like a flower, the man humming echoes the deep-throated roar of a lion,

310

awakening a power, a strength in me.

"Om-Try-Ambakam Yajaamahe
Sugandhim Pussti-Vardhanam
Urvaarukam-Iva Bandhanaan
Mrtyor-Mukssiiya Maa-mrtaat"

The mantra plays on a repeating loop and I sink deeper in Shavasana. I feel the light filtering through the window concentrating into a glowing bulb inside my forehead.

"Om, we worship the three-eyed one
Who is fragrant, increasing our nourishment
From these many bondages
May I be liberated from death
so I am not separated from the perception of immortality"

The glowing bulb grows. It swallows me whole. My entire awareness is immersed in the glow.

For a moment, I can no longer differentiate between my sense of self and the light. I am part of the light. I am light. I reconnect to the feeling from the shamanic ceremony.

My mind tunes into the frequency of eternity and I disappear.

Rajesh nudges me gently.

"Come back," he whispers.

"Holy shit, brother!" I exclaim.

"Namaste." He smiles. "I'm going to start charging you more." And we laugh.

"You know you said you thought Shiva was the destroyer of worlds..." he says.

In researching Shiva, I read that Shiva is symbolic of a great destructive force in the universe. The wind that blows down the sandcastle, the eraser on the chalkboard, the cosmic force of undoing so that creation can start again. Rajesh didn't indulge the discussion when I first asked. *There is so much for you to learn if you want to have this discussion. You haven't even read the Vedas.*

"It's not the destruction of the world. It's just the destruction of your world," he says, laughing.

I don't really know what he means, but he says it like it's a good thing and I trust him.

"Hey, Rajesh, do you guys have a lot of female gods?" He starts laughing.

"So many," he says.

"So many... many... more than male, and more powerful, even than Shiva. His wife, Parvati, some think she's more powerful than him."

I wonder about the comet that struck Earth 13,000 years ago. If that really did happen, the ice-age glaciers would have been vaporized. The world would have flooded. A cataclysm. As in the oceans moving hundreds of miles inland over an afternoon. Tsunamis the size of mountains. Raging fires and ash clouds that lasted years, maybe decades. There are tales of an apocalyptic flood in almost every ancient culture and on every continent. Most people I know are familiar with the story of Noah's Ark, but that is only one of countless stories about a great flood that destroyed the world.

If there really was an advanced society before the great flood, the traces would be hard to find, but the place for me to look is in religion. A religion that was perfect in its way of healing, unifying, and enlightening. And the signs I'd be looking for are equal symbolic weighting between male and female. The dance of yin and yang; harmony and equilibrium. In my mind, anything outside this is ignoring fundamental cosmic principles.

The regions I would look for those traces would be the Himalayan mountain ranges—high ground. Or deep inland—the Amazon basin. *The shaman and the yogis.*

I'm comforted by the way Rajesh speaks about the female Gods. The same kind of reverence and excitement as when he speaks about Shiva. My confidence in him, in this path he's guiding me along, is building. I feel like Rajesh can help guide me down the mountain, back into the world.

"Rajesh... I've been struggling with something. My work. The balance between responsibility toward my family and some of the things I need to do to compete in my world that I don't want to do anymore."

The course of my life and the feeling I have from the ceremony, that image—*the seedling*—is clashing with my ambition. My desire to compete in business and win at all costs.

I love business. The freedom of capitalism. That anyone with an idea can try and start a business, move a community forward, and take care of their family. I love the competition, the battles between companies. Competency, innovation, dedication. That's the ethical circle I'm trying to square: providing for my family and community within the context of a delicately balanced ecosystem.

"Too much for today," he says. "Next time I will tell you about the real yoga, not the one you think of."

CHAPTER 30 — WALK A LITTLE SLOWER, DAD

I check in with Mike. He's texted me a few times this week, but I've been too busy to respond.

Sorry I didn't get back to you, I text him. *I was dealing with COVID shit all week. Company is shifting into a battle stance as a few key dominoes are starting to fall.*

What kind of battle? What's COVID? he responds.

The virus. Been in crisis management mode all week. Hell of a storm coming, brother.

What kind of storm, financial?

Economic. Financial. Health. All of it, man, I answer.

Will you guys need to shift direction? I hear China is running out of money.

It's not just going to be China; this storm will be global.

I don't know. Next few days are critical. If they keep cancelling major events, we'll hit a tipping point. Supply chains are screwed. Airlines are going to lose billions.

Olympics? he asks, referring to this summer's Olympics in Japan.

Japan shut the schools down for a month. All the schools for the whole country. They shut the bike race down here in Dubai. Two of the top Italian pros had the virus, I say.

You guys shifting direction?

Direction, Mike? Read the news, brother. We are standing on a Phuket beach watching the tsunami. There is no direction.

You've always been an alarmist.

This will unfold in the next few weeks. We've never gone through this level of disruption before. Take some precautions, Mike. I've been watching this closely for two months. I didn't sound the alarm until yesterday.

COVID-19. While I was in Hong Kong, the Novel Coronavirus 2019 was breaking out in Wuhan. I've been following it a little closer than Mike because I have customers and business relationships with people in Asia and Europe that are being affected. I've been watching airport after airport slow down or shut down as the virus spreads around the world.

As viruses go, this one is set to be a Rubik's cube that we're not going to be able to figure out anytime soon.

You really are worried? he asks.

Well, my kids and parents are two continents away so there is that. The kids will be fine. My parents though. They'll be particularly vulnerable when this virus hits Canada. And it will, Mike. I was thinking of going back, but they just put out a travel advisory here warning residents to not leave or they might not easily get back in.

Doesn't sound like there's anything you can do, Mike says.

I know. I just feel like I should do something.

How's business right now? he asks.

Besides the probable total collapse of the aviation sector? Checking in on who is still at the table. We're not going to be able to get guys out to sites for a while. The parent companies are a decision cycle behind. So are the governments. It'll either be fine, really tough, or a complete disaster. So… okay?

I don't know what to say other than good luck, he says.

I am worried, but I'm also wrestling with a different part of me that isn't. That in a way, I'm just going through the motions with Mike. My heart isn't in this anymore. I don't know what constitutes good luck in this situation. A return to the status quo? In the places that are starting to shut down, pollution levels are falling to record lows and people are spending more time with their families. I'm not cheering on tragedy here—the folks losing loved ones, the doctors and nurses on the front line, families under water financially, massive unemployment... it sucks.

But feeling the effect in real time of a global slowdown, outside of the fear and anxiety, I can't help but wonder if nature is showing us a different model. *Stop running so fast.* Take a month every year and give the planet a chance to catch her breath. During Ramadan, the folks around here do something similar. A month or so per year, they work less. Focus more on each other. Take care of their bodies and community.

I feel more confusion than clarity. I still feel like I'm between assignments. Between making as much money as I can, taking care of my business and family, and whatever my heart is pulling me toward.

For now, I try and avoid the big existential questions and just focus on doing the next right thing. There is talk of a national quarantine here and Emma is supposed to be coming next week. At work, I'm still being paid to lead. I try to do that. It's going to be an interesting week.

CHAPTER 31 — YOGA

I greet Rajesh with a grumble. He greets me with open arms. We move the furniture back and lay the mats down. It's still dark outside but there is enough ambient light to practice without turning the lights on. My mood has been oscillating between peace, and the greater wisdom of slowing down, and the demands of the race. The momentum of my life, my business, and this drive to win at all costs. And this morning, I feel like I'm losing more than winning.

"Good morning!" he sings.

"Hey," I say.

"You are tired," he says.

"And angry, fearful, frustrated, sad, and confused," I respond.

"Okay, we do more pranayama," he says, cheerfully.

That's it! I don't know why I didn't think of it sooner. The last time the world had a global pandemic of this magnitude, we followed it up with a great depression and a world war not long after. The industry I work in is collapsing. The company I spent the last two decades building is facing bankruptcy. Men and women who joined our little corporate community will be kicked to the curb, livelihoods and mortgage payments disrupted. My own family dispersed, aged and ailing parents. Kids at vulnerable points in their own ascension into the world.

And Rajesh wants me to breathe through my fucking nostrils a little more.

He just smiles. He always seems to be in a good place.

I lie down on my mat. He hums and I think of chewing gum.

When the kids were a little younger and we were all living under one roof, it wasn't uncommon for me to find day-old gum in random locations. Beside a table, in the car, back of the couch, laundry basket, and so on. It's hard for me now to think about how much energy I put into trying to solve this one problem, trying to get the kids to throw their gum in the garbage. It speaks to my failings as a parent, guardian, teacher, or even adult that I could never figure out a solution. And yes, I'm ashamed. And yes, there's probably something karmic going on there because I'm sure my parents have similar versions of this story.

The day-old gum though. Not yet brittle but having lost all its elasticity and covered with the dried saliva of a feral child. That is pretty much the state of my back and hip muscles a few weeks into the sessions with Rajesh. We're making slow and steady progress. But the idea of one day being able to find a kind of ease with these asanas feels like popping that old gum into my mouth. Pretty gross and kind of pointless. I'm mildly depressed at the thought of the work ahead, and Rajesh's hymns are doing nothing for me.

I shouldn't have come this morning. I actually texted him to cancel, but I couldn't bring myself to hit send. I'm his first client. He wakes up even earlier to come out here and I think he looks forward to seeing me. Since we started the practice together, his business fortunes have significantly increased. He thinks I might be lucky in business. He's probably right.

I've managed to survive the last two decades. I've kept the lights on and the mortgages paid. Family vacations, divorce lawyers, spousal payments, private schools, parental support, and a boatload of taxes. I don't want to do it anymore. Any of it. I want to sit under a mountain or around a village campfire. Mostly I just want to be home. And I don't even know where that is anymore.

Rajesh notices my difficulty.

He knows I like discussing religion so, as if to bring me to centre, he just starts talking.

"Before we start today, we talk a little," he says. "For you, religion is about belief. For us in India, religion is seeking. It is yoga. You have to understand that when we say *yoga*, we do not mean the asanas.

The poses that you think of when you say yoga. For us, yoga means union with the divine. We seek harmony within ourselves first, then the world."

"There are different paths to union. Karma yoga is about action. Bhakti yoga is simple and devotional. It is surrender to God, to Nature, to the Cosmos. Jnana yoga is like the study of philosophy, scripture. The mind, the intellect. And this, what we are doing is one small part of Raja yoga. It is connecting the mind, body, and breath. It is meditation and self-liberation."Today, we will slow down and focus much more on pranayama, your breathing. You follow me," he says.

Sitting cross-legged, facing each other, we just breathe.

"Exhale, exhale, exhale. Imagine any toxins leaving your body. Exhale, exhale, exhale. Feel your abdomen pulsing the air out. Exhale, exhale, exhale," he says. I don't follow this as easily. The exhale is supposed to exit through my nostrils; occasionally the breath shoots through my lips.

And then we move to the retention exercise. Four seconds through one nostril. Hold for fifteen seconds. And eight seconds out through the other. My mind begins to clear and in my mind's eye, I see light.

I think about the paths of yoga.

Bhakti yoga, devotion, reverence. That pull I feel sometimes toward the exact centre of a moment, the desire to sometimes fall to my knees and look at the world with awe. The inspiration I feel of the personal Gods. For me as a boy, Jesus, his kindness and generosity of spirit. As a man, Shiva, his seeming ability to navigate the inner and outer worlds with grace and purpose.

"Innn-hale… and hold," he says over four seconds.

I did a selfless action for a stranger once. Maybe twice, but definitely at least once. I helped a guy. He called me in the middle of a busy day. I didn't particularly like him. In fact, he annoyed me to no end. Between work calls and picking the kids up from school, I was planting a tree in the garden. My hands were dirty, and I smeared mud all over my phone when I answered his call.

A friend of mine told me once that when you do something you don't want to, there's a chance it's God's will because it sure as heck isn't yours. The geometry of the universe. The gentle bend of the cosmos towards the good, that just by doing something you don't want to do, your life becomes a part of that bend. *Surrender your will and do something you don't want to do once in a while.*

I barely knew the guy who called. We met briefly on that spiritual retreat where I first met Mike. It was hard to make out over the phone, because he was crying, but I think he was suicidal. I don't know why he chose me to reach out to, but given the urgency in his voice, I didn't really think twice.

"I'll come right over," I told him.

I said it without really knowing what else to do. I was angry at him for needing my help. For being weak-minded. For interrupting my tree-planting plans and for the mud on my phone. I drove to his place and he lit up when he saw me.

"Alex! Oh my god... Alex! You look so good!" he exclaimed, which was weird because I was covered in mud.

We went into his house. It smelled of loneliness and despair. We sat at his kitchen table and he told me his woes. About his family that left him. About all that shamed him. Through tears, the man poured his heart out to me. I listened silently. I wasn't mad at him anymore. He was just a fleshy laundry basket of troubles and aspirations, fears, pain and confusion, all wet and crumpled and smelling. He was at a low point. I've had my own low points too, and for a moment, I forgot to judge him. I forgot to feel superior. I just hung out with him and every so often, he would look up. "Alex! You look so good!"

Time passed and at one point the big heave came. His shoulders sagged, his tears turned into a wave, and he wailed. I took the man into my arms. His head rested on my muddy shoulder, and I just hung out with him there too.

Eventually, I left. With a feeling that he would be okay. There would be no suicide today. And that was that. My mind was mostly empty except for a recurring image of the way he looked at me. His eyes all lit up and his refrain: *Alex! You look so good!* I was driving and I pulled over. I had to. I was overwhelmed because the answer struck me like a falling piano. He wasn't talking about my physical appearance at all. It was my presence. There at that precise moment, I wasn't a guy called Alex, I was something else. I was *hope*.

My ordinary life had been transformed and transmuted into something extraordinary. *I was hope*. And somehow that realization triggered a new awareness in me. A new level of knowledge and understanding of the world. A cosmic realization that through that one moment, I was connected to an unbroken chain of energy that stretched back to the very dawn of time. Goodness. Accidental selfless devotion. *Yoga*.

"And exxx-hale..." Rajesh sings over eight seconds.

"Through the left now innn-hale... and hold."

I've sought out and studied scripture and philosophy like a thirsty calf chasing its mother. Any and all religions and philosophers, I've consumed. Great writers and artists. Musicians and poets. In scripture and philosophy, I found that occasional eye-opening moment. I have connected through time to wisdom. *Yoga*.

We release and inhale one more time.

My mind's eye is empty. No vision. Just a warm emptiness. I feel a sense of gratitude building inside me. I feel connected to Rajesh and this moment. I feel my lips curling gently into a smile. I am finding my path between the heavens and the earth. My union between the divine and this world. *Raja yoga*.

Karma yoga though. Karma yoga is the trickiest for me.

I've heard lots of stories about karma. It's Newton's third law: Every action has an equal and opposite reaction. It's the symmetry of nature. If I put violence and hatred into the world, that same energy will come back toward me. It's not morality, it's physics. Maybe not as mathematical as Newtonian mechanics because the world is a big place, but the operational principles are the same.

In the emptiness, I feel a sense of my karma, the accumulated transactions between me and the world and what I need to do to bring it into equilibrium. I narrow every single transaction I've ever had with the world into a single relationship. That's my karma. *I took more than I gave in this relationship.*

The race I've been running has to change.

From conquest and dominion toward equilibrium within myself and empowerment of others around me. It's not a race for me anymore; it's a slow walk from the outer edge of a spinning wheel to the very centre, a walk toward harmony. I don't need to run as fast anymore. I never did; the arc of nature in equilibrium bends toward the good and plenty.

Rajesh puts his hands together in a prayer position and starts chanting. I put my hands together. I don't follow him in the chanting because I don't know the words, but I chime in at the end.

"Shanti... Shanti... Shanti..."

Peace... Peace... Peace...

Rajesh smiles at me. I smile back. I feel the gentle curl of my lip and the shine in my eyes. *Yoga*. I feel deeply rooted in cosmic gratitude. *I breathe.*

CHAPTER 32 — ZIPLINE

Emma arrived last night. She's only staying for a few days on spring break. This might be one of the last times we see each other for a while. National quarantines are becoming standard practice as the virus spreads, and judging by the infection numbers here, we might only be a few weeks away from a lockdown.

She wants to see and do as much as possible. When I get in from a morning walk, she is already up and sitting on the couch. Nancy is making breakfast.

"Can we go ziplining today?" she asks.

The session yesterday with Rajesh left me lighthearted and in a state of saying yes to things I wouldn't otherwise. I'm not a thrill seeker. Flying down a cable suspended across a desert cityscape is not in my nature, but it is in hers and I want to be closer to her. I miss her. I've missed the closeness. The trust and the intimacy. Watching her grow and blossom. I just wish there were better ways of doing that right now.

"Sure," I answer.

"Really?" she says.

"Yeah, I want to do this with you."

"Really?" Nancy chimes in from behind the counter.

Nancy and Emma laugh.

I'm surprised by how surprised they are but, then again, I probably shouldn't be. From Emma's point of view, all her life I've been the kind of dad who is busy, distant, at times angry, stressed, frustrated, and, on the rare occasion, present and loving. From my point of view, I've been focused on keeping things together and trying my very best to give the kids a platform they can build their lives on.

Rajesh has helped bring me toward the centre of my own life. To bring my thoughts and actions in line with my experiences at the shaman ceremony. If I don't quite yet know what to do in terms of specifics, I feel at least like I have the tools to get to an answer. With Emma, Jesse, and Amelia though, it's harder.

I still feel a sense of urgent concern about the world they are entering. The community back home. The pandemic is only amplifying this feeling. Wisdom about right action or right thought eludes me, and short of that, I hide out in the present. I try to be fully present to Emma for the short amount of time she will be here.

#

We arrive at the zipline kiosk inside a shopping mall. The young man inside the kiosk is way too happy to see us.

"You are here for an adventure today!" he exclaims.

"Yes!" Emma says.

"Fantastic! Sir, how much do you weigh?" he asks.

I weigh just under two hundred and go-fuck-yourself pounds.

"I'm under the maximum limit," I tell him.

"Of course. But just for safety, could you please weigh yourself in front of me here?"

As if jumping off a building wasn't enough. A public reminder of the last few years of undisciplined and emotional eating between the healthy diet regimens with Nancy.

"This is funny for you," I say, looking at Emma.

She's laughing too hard to answer.

"Sir, keep your weight the same and you can enjoy this adventure anytime you want," the young man says, cheerily.

We arrive at the base of a skyscraper overlooking the marina. We make our way to the fifty-plus story rooftop. *This is insane.*

Along the way, a bright and smiling guy from the Philippines explains what's about to happen.

"Once we are at the top, you will have a chance to take some pictures. Once you are ready, we will strap you to the harness and walk you to the ledge. Here you will lie down and we will make final adjustments. The total ride is one kilometre. Maybe fifty seconds. For the first few seconds, please keep your hands on the harness, but after you can stretch out your hands and fly like Superman. Okay?"

"Okay!" Emma exclaims.

At the top, time slows. The warmth of the rising desert air. The blue sky. The outline of the sandy, palm-shaped island set against the green hues of the Arabian Gulf. We are above the skyline, looking down on incredible architecture and feats of engineering. And in the middle of it all, Emma, the heart that walks outside my chest, is happy, excited, exhilarated, and grateful.

We take photos. A man with a video camera films us. We speak briefly into a camera. The men by the ledge attach the cables and walk us to the platform. We lie down beside each other a dozen feet apart, and for a few seconds, I avoid looking down. I don't have a fear of heights as much as a fear of doing dumb things. But I'm focused on Emma. I'm committed. I want to execute this as gracefully as I can.

No daughter should have to see their dad curled up in a wet ball of fear, as tempting as that sounds to me right now.

"Sweetie, all those moments I let you down, this wipes the slate clean, okay?" I shout.

"Okay!" she shouts back, laughing.

"Three, two, one, go!" a voice behind us shouts.

I'm flying more than I'm falling. Directly below me is the canal that leads to the marina. Behind me is Emma. I hear her shouts of exhilaration.

Time slows even more and fifty seconds becomes fifty minutes.

I see the high-rise offices and apartments. I look inside kitchens and office cubicles. I feel the air, the wind.

Her shouts of delight are getting closer to me.

I think about the first tooth fairy and all those moments I came up short as a dad. Lost moments. A young adult's lifetime's worth. They sting; they add up. And sometimes they create a map of a frustrated, busy, and anxious world . The world of bullshit and made-up things.

But that's not the world. It's just one place on the map. And in the slowtime of the flying, I feel the proximity of wisdom and clarity. It's an ethereal presence. A genie out of its bottle.

Great Genie, how do I become a better father?

Be more present with your kids.

Emma is beside me now, arms outstretched, flying past me like Superwoman.

She is laughing. She is experiencing and discovering… a different version of the man she grew up with. We are entering uncharted territory, a new place on the map of her world.

#

It's Emma's last day. We try and squeeze in a little bit of culture with a visit to the Grand Mosque in Abu Dhabi.

I watched a lot of action movies growing up. The heroes changed but the bad guys were usually the same. Bad guy Soviets or bad guy Arabs. In the movies with the bad guy Arabs, the call to prayer was ominous and the mosques were central stations, headquarters for nefarious action and bad intention.

"It's not what I thought," Emma says.

"I know, right?" I say.

We are outside the mosque. The call to prayer is playing. Hearing it at the same time as taking in the sight of the mosque is arresting.

"Let's find a place to sit," I say.

I just want to get on my knees.

"The veil really suits you," I tell her.

She's wearing a violet hijab provided by the mosque.

"Don't get used to it," she says.

"I know. It's just that… five more minutes. Just give your old Pops five more minutes," I say.

"I don't get it, why the women have to wear this," she says.

"I know."

Just five more minutes seeing her this way. For her it might be a regressive practice, but for me right now it's dignity and reverence. The veil just highlights her beauty in a way the yoga pants and tank top don't.

We listen to a man singing the call to prayer. I don't know the words. Maybe it's better that way because I just feel the stirring inside me. The same stirring I felt occasionally at midnight mass growing up, or when visiting Angkor Wat. The magnetic pull of divinity, of sacred spaces, people, and moments.

Untethered love and inspiration. It's not something I can manufacture or trap. It doesn't stay in one place. We crept up on it, a little bit of ritual, a hijab for Emma and my Sunday best. My internal compass stops spinning and settles on north. The song pulls me in. The mosque, the soft edges of the qubba and the tranquility of the sahn. The gold-tipped minarets and Emma, her eyes shining bright as though lit from within.

I've never been inside during the prayers. But I've seen my friends prepare. Washing their hands, feet, and face. Cleansing themselves to pray.

"Sometimes at work here I'll be in a meeting. And the guy at the meeting says we have to stop. That it's the call to prayer and off he goes. I sit and wait for him to come back. And when he does, he's a little different. He looks at me a little differently. Things slow down and it just feels so…"

Emma smiles. "Feels what?" she asks.

"Human," I say.

She nods.

"Thank you," I say.

"For what?" she asks.

"The five minutes," I say.

#

We are getting ready to head out. Emma's big pink suitcase is packed. She's been quiet all afternoon. I know what's coming because I feel it too.

She walks out of the room, rolling her suitcase behind her.

"Are you all ready?" Nancy asks.

Emma doesn't speak. She just nods. She can't speak and I can't either.

Nancy gives her a hug and they hold each other without saying anything.

The tears are welling inside me. The inside of my cheek is bleeding.

I move to her suitcase and start pulling it toward the door.

"Bye Emma, safe flight," Nancy says.

Emma nods.

The drive to the airport is quiet. Love is so close to the surface for both of us. I feel so close to her, so connected. I don't want her to go, and she doesn't want to leave.

At the airport, I take her suitcase out of the truck and walk her to the door. We stand outside and I take her in my arms. The dams burst. The tears come pouring out. Both of us. I don't want to let her go and she doesn't want to let go. If there's cruelty in love, I feel it in this moment.

"Text me when you get through security, okay?" I whisper in her ear.

She walks away without looking back. Her big pink suitcase rolls along behind her. My heart disappears behind the departure doors of Dubai airport.

CHAPTER 33 — PETIT PRINCE

The government here announced the lockdown will be starting next week. I bought tickets for the opera tonight. It might be our last outing for a while.

There's been a little tension between Nancy and me since the shaman ceremony. I'd like to think it's just because of the virus and the general stress of the move and a new environment, but part of me worries that it's deeper. That our paths might be diverging. The practice with Rajesh has helped; I feel reconnected with myself but still a pull away from this life. I don't fully understand it. A resonant dissonance inside me that I need to live differently, and Nancy wants stability.

Whatever it is, tonight will be a nice distraction.

One of our first dates together was at the opera. It was my first time. She had dressed up, high heels and refined elegance. She was excited. Me, not so much. I was happy that she was happy. There are some new experiences that I look forward to, but sitting for a couple of hours in a theatre full of people who like opera was not one of them.

I jumped in the driver's seat and waited for Nancy to get in. She was standing outside the passenger door for what seemed like a long time. I looked over but she didn't look at me. I got out of the car to see if maybe her heel was stuck or the door was jammed. When I reached her side, she just looked at me strangely. She wasn't giving me any clues, so it took me a while to realize that she was waiting for me to open the passenger door for her.

Date night. A little bit of chivalry was required. Message transmitted; message received.

Tonight, Nancy is wearing black. Skirt and sweater, high heels. We walk toward the car and I open the door for her. She smiles. It's still not often I do that. Not often enough. Her appreciation embarrasses me. Such a small act, so easy, and I do it so seldom.

The Dubai Opera house is contemporary but feels old world at the same time. Glass, steel, with rich wood grain. The theatre boxes look like small wooden galleys. Beautifully carved, floating up the wall. The curtain is deep, lush red. The room is packed with beautiful people, well adorned and heeled. There's a sense of occasion.

The show is mostly dancing. "The Little Prince." A few spoken words from the book but the attention is on the movement of the people on stage. The yellow-haired man descending from the stage to stand on a small, planet-shaped ball. He walks on the ball and rolls it beneath his feet, moving around a stage as though it wasn't an impossible feat for anyone watching.

From the side of the stage a lady reads aloud: "And now here is my secret, a very simple secret: It is only with the heart that one can see rightly; what is essential is invisible to the eye."

People dressed as white sheep move around the young man with yellow hair. I still strain to be present at these shows. I try watching through Nancy's eyes and I see the slowness of their movement. The yoga practice has awakened my body and I can, in their movement, see the very outer limits of what the body is capable of. Lithe and alive they move, expressing a kind of beauty that Nancy and the rest of the room seem to melt into.

The lady speaks again: "A rock pile ceases to be a rock pile the moment a single man contemplates it, bearing within him the image of a cathedral." My mind drifts to this city, Dubai, where a man not so long ago contemplated some sand dunes and a rock pile. He saw this cathedral of wood, steel, sound, and colour and a vibrant city around it. A life, a rockpile, and a dream.

I stray in and out of presence until a new lady appears on the stage. I can't see her face, only red silk in motion. She moves in a way that traps me in the moment. I am transfixed, mesmerized.

From where I sit, I can only see her outline. Her colour changes with her dance, from red into yellow and back; a rose in the sunlight.

Time slows. The man beside her on the stage is trapped in the same moment as me. We gaze. We witness.

Until the movement stops, the lights dim, and in unison the crowd claps. Perfectly synchronized.

"Faites que le rêve dévore votre vie afin que la vie ne dévore pas votre rêve."
The lady speaks and the show ends.

Nancy and I walk out of the opera hand in hand. "Perfect timing!" she says, as in front of us an explosion of lights, music, and water jets from the Dubai Mall fountain seems cued up for our exit.

I'm in a moment of profound appreciation for the perfection of this, here, now. For Nancy, glowing beside me. The cathedral in the desert. The present state of health and well-being of everyone I know and love. It's all. Just. Perfect. Like a dream.

For the briefest of moments, I get a strange feeling. It's an odd thought that I've had just a few times in my life and only since I left Maui seven years ago. Sometimes I wonder if I'm still in Maui in the middle of a painful and costly divorce and that this is all a dream.

Or maybe something happened on my trip up the volcano and the life I knew ended. Like the end of a movie where you realize the guy was dead the whole time and everyone watching goes *"Ohhhh... of course!"*

Because it all feels so perfect to me.

"The woman in red and yellow," Nancy says, looking at me.

"Moving, eh?" I say.

She nods, takes my hand, and we walk.

CHAPTER 34 — QUARANTINE

Since the quarantine started Rajesh and I don't do the yoga sessions anymore, but we keep in touch.

I give him a call.

"Namaste, brother," I say.

"Good morning, brother," he says.

"Shiva," I say.

"Yes?"

"He destroyed my world."

I don't know if some Hindu God really destroyed my world, but my business has been decimated and a big part of my world for the past two decades has been that business. Six months ago, this would have devastated me. I don't feel that way right now. What I feel—this strange new sensation—is liberation.

"Congratulations, brother."

I feel like Rajesh could see through me from the beginning. That he knew exactly what I needed and the confidence that life is unfolding in just the right way. That's the skill of the yogi. Less to teach and more just to be present to the unfolding of a life. With a little water, earth, and sunlight, the acorn grows into an oak, like a boy becomes a man.

"What happens now?" I ask.

"Keep breathing," he says.

And I laugh into the phone.

"Whenever I do the practice now, I'm starting to feel... home," I say.

Rajesh laughs.

"Good. But you still have one hundred and eleven more techniques to learn."

"What do you mean?"

"Shiva's wife once asked him how to fully be realized in this world. To be fully awake, connected to this reality and the other. He told her that there were one hundred and twelve ways."

"Why a hundred and twelve?"

"That's what she said. She got mad. She said there should be more. So, she went looking for more."

"Did she find any?"

"No. If she did, there would be one hundred and thirteen," he says, laughing.

"I miss our sessions, man," I tell him. "I'm looking forward to seeing you again. When this is all over, can we go to India together? To Kailash, Mansarovar? Visit the temples and the sadhus. I want to learn more about the female aspect of divinity."

"Yes, brother, yes. I have never visited so much of my country. Yes. Let's do that together. But for now, try to keep your practice while we are in quarantine. Keep your progress," he says.

"How does it feel to be a husband and father again?" I ask him. His wife and daughter arrived from India a few days ago. Last flight into the country.

"So happy!" he says.

"I'm so happy for you, brother, your God is taking care of you," I say, and he laughs like a man free of all worry. I can relate. There was a time in my life where everyone I cared about could fit on the same queen-size mattress. The people I care about now span continents.

#

I check the international clock on my phone for the current time in Maui. I'm going to call Fadi. The US is living through a chaotic period. Shutdowns, intense debate about masks and freedom. The odd contrast of socially distanced street protests.

"Brother, how are you doing?" I ask.

"I'm better, man. It's been a rough week. Things look to be stabilizing, but I still feel like we're a little lost," he says.

It's been a rough few years for the good people of America and even greater challenges on the horizon.

"This might not mean much to you right now, but I envy your green card," I say.

As a Canadian, I grew up with mixed feelings about the US. Like a couple in a restaurant talking loudly about the problems in their marriage, it's hard not to pay attention. Maybe make a judgement or two about who is right and who is wrong. To sit at my table in smug condemnation of *their* problems. But having lived and worked in a lot of different nations, it's a little easier to see that, for the most part, the problems are all the same for everyone. Nobody has this twenty-first century figured out yet.

America. Barely 250 years. Four generations. And yet so much history. Cruelty and kindness, generosity and greed, wisdom and foolishness, freedom and oppression. So much, *life*. The sheer audacity of the dreams of self-governing free people and Martin Luther King's dream of sons of former slaves and sons of former slave owners coming together.

Charles Manson, the Zodiac Killer, the Vietnam War, and various protests and riots were all going on at the same time as Woodstock and the Moon landings. *America.*

"What was that place we went hiking... the big canyon on the other island?" I ask.

"Waimea Canyon... Kauai," he says.

"Jurassic Park," I say.

I remember walking along the cliff edge of that canyon.

"Remember that burger joint in DC you brought me to?"

Fadi laughs. "Fuddruckers."

I celebrated Cinco de Mayo in New Mexico just before Emma was born. When she was barely a month old, I drove her to LA. She was in my arms for the Fourth of July fireworks. She was in a stroller on Santa Monica pier when I looked out toward Malibu. We watched the sunset over the Pacific.

I was in DC for the night of the 2008 presidential election.

I drove across the country. From San Diego through the California Chocolate Mountains and the Mojave Desert to El Paso. Across Texas. Through Texarkana to Buffalo with stops in Nashville and Ohio. I walked in Central Park and had a hot dog in Yankee Stadium. I watched Jesse play hockey in Boston and upstate New York. I sat on Daytona Beach and watched the space shuttle light up the evening sky.

So much freedom.

I've never been to Mount Rushmore, but I've seen pictures of the founding fathers carved into the rock. I've seen the Statue of Liberty. The woman and the torch, standing on the edge of the country, and I imagine her gently drawing the gaze of the founding fathers toward the rising sun. *Tomorrow will be better than today.*

I believe in the dream. *That one day…*

"Not lost, man, just trying to find the way," I say.

"It doesn't feel that way right now," he says. "At all."

"How's Noah doing?" I ask.

"He's good, man. It was his second birthday a few weeks ago. Cath and I set up a treasure hunt. All over the house, he found little gifts and clues. We hid the big gift in my office. He found it last. You know what he says to me when he finds it?"

"What?"

"Dad! Dad! You are so lucky. Look at that toy castle in your office!"

"You've been blessed, brother."

"I know. It's just hard sometimes to feel that way with everything going on."

"You care, man. Caring about the world is painful, but occasionally, amid the chaos and the cruelty, you see something, you feel something. So beautiful. So inspiring, and you feel the pull... That's the thing you have to grab on to. True North," I say.

"There was a guy last week. A sheriff at a protest. He took off his helmet. Put down his baton. He spoke with the protestors. He told them he wanted to turn the protest into a parade. They shouted *Walk with us. Walk with us.* And they did. They walked together... I liked that," he says.

... That one day... The nation will rise up and live out the true meaning if its creed... That one day on the red hills of Georgia the sons of former slaves and the sons of former slave owners will be able to sit down together at the

table of brotherhood...

In the long shadow cast by thousands of years of monarchy and tyranny, war and genocide around the world, a nation of immigrants, sons of slaves and former slave owners, strives toward an ideal. That all men are created equal, that they are endowed by their creator with certain unalienable rights, that among these are life, liberty and the pursuit of happiness. The audacious dream and the courage to even try. *America.*

Even when falling short of the ideal, there is beauty in the striving. *Keep striving, Fadi.*

"Aloha, brother," he says.

Aloha, Fadi.

CHAPTER 35 — PALE BLUE EGG

I bring a few berries with me outside and leave them on the edge of the balcony. The mynas now always have their mouths open. At first, I thought it was because they were always hungry, but Nancy told me it's how they deal with the heat. I might have been overfeeding them because one is looking a little heavy on his feet. *Easy on the berries, Buds. You can fly but you still have to land.*

My friends in North America and Europe are quiet these days. I reach out to them and receive only one- or two-word answers. The world is in a timeout. Mike, drained of his exuberance and strength, cuts a sad figure over the messaging, so I give him a call.

"Something I realized last night," I tell him. "Never in recorded history have so many people on this planet felt the same way you and I do right now."

"I don't find that comforting," Mike says.

"Seriously, you okay?" I ask.

"A little unsettled. Nothing to do with this exact moment as much as preparing for stage two."

Nobody knows what stage two is. Governments have injected massive amounts of money into the central banking system. There's an asset bubble of historic proportions. Protests in the streets around the world about injustice and inequality. Once marginal conspiracy theories are becoming mainstream, institutional trust is deteriorating, and our climate is changing. Tensions in the South China Sea rise almost daily. Scientists have brought forward the doomsday clock; it's 100 seconds from midnight, the closest we've ever been to nuclear annihilation since the clock's inception in 1947.

But I'm optimistic.

"I'm optimistic. Maybe stage two… maybe this transformation is bringing us to a better place. There are dolphins in the canals of Venice," I say.

"You think shutting down the global economy to see dolphins swimming in canals is progress?"

"Maybe. They do it here for Ramadan every year."

"They don't shut everything down."

"No, but they reduce working hours. They slow down. They focus on each other, their families, their communities. The people in need around them. The work will be there when they get back. They just take a month for each other. The whole country, all at once. I like that."

It's not just the dolphins. There are other bright spots. Italians singing to each other on balconies. Deer on the streets of Paris. Parts of the Himalayas are now visible to cities in India for the first time in decades.

It's a little easier for me to be upbeat. I've been lucky so far. I haven't been impacted directly by the pandemic, other than financially. And amid the chaos, I feel a sense of hope that the future—that whatever the world looks like coming out of this period—will be better than the world that went in. Maybe not right away, maybe not for a while, but there's a brighter tomorrow coming.

As businessmen, Mike and I have found a little humility. Ship captains on sinking boats. Not a lot of captaining to do once you accept that whatever happens next is completely outside your control. Mike is downbeat though.

"In the last five thousand years, man can't seem to ever get it right. We always say the new generation is worse. I think we don't really start getting life until we live it. I think we find out when it's too late. Maybe our last breath. I know it's within me. Around me. In the rocks and the flowers and the mountains and the sky and the animals and all the living things. And if I can love them, I will find what has always been there... Or something like that."

"Mike, we say the new generation is always better, not worse. Evolution brings us forward not backward."

"Does it? I'd say it's worse."

Mike gets the last word and we laugh a little at the silliness of the argument.

We are laughing but I sense his grief. The simultaneous grasping and letting go. The polarity of accepting defeat and fighting until the last breath.

"Mike, you ever heard of the Eleusinian mysteries?" I ask.

"Ah, buddy, where are you going now? No. I have no idea," he replies.

"Nowhere. I've just been wondering about something."

"What's that?"

"Where did all the books on the feminine aspect of religion and divinity go?"

Around the period of the rise of the Roman Empire, the Greeks were known to have a sacred ritual that involved plants and Demeter, Goddess of the land and the harvest. Rituals that in the abstract read very much like the shaman ceremonies of the Amazon. But the history and specifics of the ritual were lost to time and war. Temples were destroyed and only historic trace elements remain. Hence the mystery.

"Which books?"

"Exactly. It's the Eleusinian mysteries and not the Eleusinian scriptures. Same thing about Angkor Wat. Go try and find out what was going on there with all those women Goddesses holding plants by their womb. It was only a few hundred years ago we were hanging women and calling them witches for taking part in rituals outside the lines of the church."

"It's always been that way."

"I think you're wrong. The people who built the Great Pyramid. The society that designed Angkor Wat. I think that might have been a society in balance, in harmony with itself. Between man and woman, the inner world of religion and wisdom and the outer world of science and knowledge," I say.

"That makes you optimistic?" he says.

"Not in the slightest. What makes me optimistic is that I met a priest who showed me unity and taught me about love. I met a shaman who totally transformed my way of looking at the world. She practiced witchcraft on me, Mike. She made me care about Earth and the people in it more than my own glory. And I met a yogi who helped me bring that awareness, the reverence for the world into my daily life. I found religion, Mike. True religion, brother, it's out there.

"I think maybe that's what the Eleusinian rites were about. Connecting people to Demeter, the earth. Fertility and Sacred Law. That once upon a time we had a way of living together in harmony with each other and the land. This whole time I thought I needed to reconnect with what my grandad had. The old church, his religion. I don't think that anymore. My grandma couldn't even vote when they got married. Nancy's grandma was excommunicated because she refused to have more than thirteen kids. I don't need to reconnect with that past. There's a better future coming.

"Things are changing, Mike. Destruction is the prelude to creation. We may be witnessing the birth of a new epoch. The dying gasps of the warrior king and his lineage of sons into something new, something better. Sons and daughters. Harmony, with each other and the land."

"I think you're a little nuts," he says.

"Maybe. But think about that. You think I'm nutty for believing that a world in harmony, that takes care of the planet and each other, is a real possibility in our lifetime."

Amidst the chaos of the world, the ignorance and passion, there is still goodness.

"I'm glad you're happy but I don't share your optimism. Things aren't looking so good here. And I gotta run, buddy," Mike says.

"Hey, before you go, did I tell you I'm running a bird nursery now?"

"You mean an aviary?" he says.

"Yeah, that. Found an eggshell. I think the myna's had a baby," I say.

I found half an eggshell on the balcony yesterday. The size of half my thumb. Tiny and blue. Topaz.

"A chick. And probably not. Probably some other bird ate their egg and spat the shell out on your balcony," he says.

"Jesus, Mike, I like my version better."

"I have to get to work... one day at a time," he says.

"Love you, brother," I say.

I put the phone down and think about my beautiful friend Mike.

He has been a pillar for me in my temple of manhood. Stoic and unchanging. He held things together for me long enough to rebuild.

#

My mom and I have got closer these past few months. She's not much of a talker over the phone but she likes writing. We talk over WhatsApp semiregularly now. She's worried about Nancy and me out here. I'm worried about her over there.

Occasionally, I send her a picture of the sunset. "Sending the sun over to you" and she sends me things she's reading to pass the time in quarantine. She shares a little more about her life. Turns out my interest in Hindu mysticism might have been inherited. She tells me stories about the '60s. The Beatles and the yogis.

I keep that photo of the sunset in a folder on my phone. There's another picture in that directory and it's of my parents. Together. Nancy and I went back to Canada for Christmas and my parents spent Christmas day together.

It was my mom's idea. I picked her up Christmas Day morning and brought her to the lake. The kids and Emma were driving down separately, picking my dad up along the way. It was going to be a surprise. Nancy was in the kitchen preparing a feast. We hadn't had a Christmas Day together in years.

I heard Emma's car pulling up. I looked up the snowy driveway and watched the girls rush down the slope toward the door.

"Nana!" they exclaimed.

They ran to my mom and embraced her.

My dad walked slow. He was holding on to Jesse's arm. They inched along. I waited in anticipation. *Merry Christmas, Pop.*

Jesse opened the door.

"Nana!" he exclaimed.

My dad followed him and saw Mom. His mouth was open. He was stunned.

She took him in her arms. They held each other. Long enough for me to take a picture. For her to whisper something in his ear and for him to open his mouth even wider.

My dad looked at me, confused. Happy and confused.

"She's so beautiful," he said.

I smiled and gave him a hug.

"Did you know?" he asked.

"Yeah, Pop... yeah, I did... Merry Christmas," I said.

I think of my mom in her basement flat. The quarantine is hard on her. Winter is always tough in Canada, but the added stress of a virus that is particularly dangerous for the elderly, along with complete isolation, is taking its toll. Her messages are getting further apart. Her flame in this world is sputtering. She's made peace with her relatives, long since passed. She's let go of the anger and resentment, the old grudges buried deep within her.

She calls my dad once in a while now just to let him know he's cared for.

I send her a picture of the sunset. "Sending the sun over to you."
Spring is coming, Mom, hang in there.

#

Amelia doesn't text me often. She sends me GIFs, short one- or two-second video clips. She says they express more feelings than can be described in words. She's right.

I started sending them back to her. Usually whatever is the most random one I can find. Tonight, it's a hamster waving hello.

Her school is online now and she's managing well. She lets me know how good her grades are before she tells me the news.

"I'm living with my boyfriend BTW... until quarantine is over... I forgot to tell you," she says.

I resend her the GIF of the hamster waving hello.

Raising Amelia is mostly just staying out of her way and cheering from the sidelines.

She is indomitable. Once, aged somewhere between a baby and a toddler, she was running around naked after a bath. I brought out a pull-up diaper for her to put on and handed it to her. She threw the diaper right back at me. Confused and irritated, I gently tapped her bum cheek. *That was rude, put on the diaper.* She was indignant and threw the diaper back at me even harder. I spanked her again. It escalated until we reached a point of capitulation and surrender. *Okay, you don't need to wear diapers anymore.*

Lately we've been arguing. I use the term loosely. More like me pleading with her about course selection for university.

She wants to focus on gender studies and sociology. I'm trying to make a case for business and law. She likes both but is leaning toward the former.

"What's wrong with sociology and gender studies? It's science and you like science," she asked.

"It might be science one day but right now it's just ideology."

"You don't know what you're talking about. I want to help people," she said.

"I know, that's why I think law and business is the best path."

I struggle to translate for her what I intuit. That the tools of sociology and psychology today are rudimentary. That our collective domain proficiency, our understanding of a human being, is verging on primitive. The level of knowledge of our own minds is one that should urge humility, not confidence.

We are, however, exceptionally skilled at industrial and technological power. We have figured out how to blow up a planet and burn it to the ground. And plenty of good things too. I want my daughter to learn about the kind of capitalism that doesn't make the headlines, the one where free people have ideas, get together, and solve problems.

"We both know you're going to do whatever you want, so I guess thank you for at least asking what I think, but before you make a decision, google Jessica Jackley and Jacqueline Novogratz," I said.

I tell her about two inspirational leaders in the world of business that I admire.

"But know this, whatever you end up doing, I'll be in your cheering section."

#

The world is changing quickly. Being stripped naked and laid bare. There's a toilet paper shortage.

Jesse was supposed to fly over in a couple of days. I get a text from him saying he's worried and he's not sure if he still wants to come.

I just don't want to die at 17, he says.

He's afraid. Normally, I would have consoled him. Given him solace. That the world is going to mostly be okay. Except this time, I don't. Partly because he's a man now, I need to respect that space. And partly because I don't know what 'okay' means anymore and that's just fine. *Jesse, sleep on it and trust your instincts. You're a man now and I love you. In Dubai or in Canada I love you,* I tell him.

His mother is worried also. I miss him deeply, but imagining the young man and his mother, caring for one another during the storm, makes me smile. I cancel his flight.

Next, I call my dad, which I always have to do twice before he answers. The first time he usually fumbles around trying to find his phone then can't quite get the swiping right before the rings run out. The second time he picks up by the third ring.

"Pop!"

"Alexander!"

"How are you?"

"Excellent."

"Really? You're not too worried about the virus?" I ask.

"I have enough problems to worry about. I don't have time for viruses."

"Have they changed anything at the home?"

"They locked us all in our rooms. We can't go downstairs for dinner anymore. I did lose two friends."

"From the virus?"

"No. One guy fell and broke his hip. He went to the hospital and then they said he had cancer. The other guy just got really old. Ninety-eight, I think."

"Jesus. Sorry to hear that, Pop."

"They were good men. But old."

"You doing okay though, seriously?"

"I miss your mom, but she's been calling me every once in a while and we talk. I'm worried about these cell phone charges but I'm like a broken record with all that, I know."

I've told him at least a dozen times it doesn't cost him anything when I call but it doesn't stick. But hearing about my mom calling him warms my heart.

"I'll keep it short, Pop. I just wanted to tell you I love you. I've been meditating a lot about our family lately."

"Meditating? Ah shit. You're not Catholic anymore?"

He says it in the same tone he used when I told him about my first tattoo. My poor dad, worried about changes in his boy that he doesn't understand. I'm smiling.

"I'm a lot of things, Pop."

Just to avoid stressing him out, I don't tell him about the yoga.

"Did you get the money transfer?" I ask.

"I can't figure out how to deposit it. I think the bank changed my password."

"Okay. I'll ask Emma to give you a hand. Do you need anything else, Pop, anything I can do?"

"Just hearing the sound of your voice, son. That's good enough for me. How's your work?"

"I'm not sure. It's pretty chaotic but I'm not worried anymore."

"You think it's all going to work out?"

"Something is going to work out. I just don't know what that means and I'm not too worried about it anymore. Nancy and the kids are good. Friends are good."

"Did you see any camels?"

"I saw some camels, Pop. I'll take some pictures and send you some next time."

"Don't send them to me. I can't figure out how to open them. Send them to one of the kids."

"Okay, Pop. I'm going to go to bed here, it's getting late. I just wanted to tell you that I love you."

"I love you too, son, thanks for calling."

Sleep well, Pops.

CHAPTER 36 — LO, RADIANT ONE

Nancy and I are in bed. Weeks into the quarantine, we have a bit of a routine. She's been working from home. I mostly do yoga and meditate. This is the longest I've gone in my life without being productive. Without building or inventing, selling or managing. I've barely been consuming either and somehow, for right now, I feel I've contributed as much to the world through inaction than all my years of working. The planet needed a break and, I think, so did I.

I've changed these past few months and the *new me* is straining our relationship. The tension between us has been building since I first told her about wanting to go visit a shaman. We've spoken about it but never much beyond the surface, neither of us fully ready to explore the implications of what this change could mean.

I've been struggling trying to fully integrate my experience from the ceremony. After the ceremony, a part of me wanted Nancy to drop everything in her life and plant gardens and design temples. When the pandemic started, I had an urge to build an ark. To find a patch of land and bring everyone I cared about there and hide from the growing chaos in the world. I do not yet feel a sense of clarity about my own impulses and drive.

To my friends and family, I try to project as much optimism as I can muster. But inside, I'm still a little confused. About the world and my role in it. I thought about becoming a yogi. Or maybe with enough training, a shaman. Maybe take a little hiatus and try life as a sadhu. None of that quite fits with being a devoted husband and the wedding vows I took. I've been putting off talking to Nancy about how I feel until I had a sense of clarity, but it can't wait any longer. Absent clarity I shoot for honesty.

"I wanted to talk to you about something," I say.

She gives me a worried look. Something about my tone.

"When this is over, I'm not going back to the business."

"I had a feeling. All this religious stuff…"

There's a crispness in her expression. Not quite angry but there are some high voltage wires nearby.

"I feel like I know what you might be thinking," I say.

"And what would that be?"

"That you didn't sign up to marry a religious freak… and that not even a year ago we agreed on a three-year plan," I say.

She doesn't answer.

"I'm not going to shave my head or let go of my responsibilities. I'm just not going back to *that* business. First of all, I have no idea when global aviation will look anything like it did in two thousand and nineteen, but more than that. I tell the kids to focus on what inspires them, problems around them they can help solve, and I don't follow my own advice. Helping airports get more capacity out of a runway isn't a problem that needs solving anymore," I say.

"When you told me about the shaman, I didn't like it, but I was supportive. When you told me about the Hindu stuff—I get it. That's you. You're curious. You want to learn everything there is to know about a subject. I love that about you. But you're also responsible. You're a dad. You're my husband. And you're rational. I don't understand all this religious stuff... Where are you going with this?" she pleads.

"I don't know, but I want you to come with me. I want to show you what I saw, what I experienced. I want you to see *that world*..." I trail off.

"I don't want to see *that* world! I want you to come back and be with me in this one!"

Okay, now she's angry.

"There is so much pain here. So much confusion. That elephant we saw in Cambodia, suffering—" I say before she cuts me off.

"We didn't just see a suffering elephant in Cambodia... We saw a good man, working hard, caring for it!"

Nancy, my beautiful wife, has this way of framing things sometimes. This uncanny ability to elegantly and ever so gracefully hit me on the side of a head with a silk-covered brick. To emphatically steer me toward a moment of clarity.

My face must have registered what I'm feeling because her eyes soften a little. I try and speak but I'm confused.

"I just... I don't know. I try to be optimistic, but it all just feels so wrong right now," I say. "So broken. Like we lost the instruction manual for how these bodies and minds are supposed to operate. Our community... falling apart. The way I see people sometimes, it's like watching a man trying to wash his clothes with a lawnmower. I try to ignore it because it's none of my business and I'm the last person to be giving advice, but there is a better way," I say.

"Whatever it is you think you know, you can't push it on people."

"I know..."

The sadhu's life can't be for me. I always knew that, of course. Before everything else, I'm a father and husband, but there's a part of me that is burning inside. I don't know what to do with that part.

"What are you going to do?" she asks.

"I don't know."

I feel a little deflated. Because of all the people I wish I could share what I saw and felt during the ceremony, it's her.

Learning about Shiva from Rajesh, what I found most interesting about the stories, about this mystical yogi, is that he was in love. The Shiva Sutras, the writings attributed to him, are basically just a love letter to his consort. That, however profound the beauty might be on the other side of the veil, it wasn't worth a single wordless breath if he couldn't share it with her.

Lo, Radiant one…

The Shiva Sutras. His 112 ways. The yogi wrote his beloved a love letter and shared it with the world.

A thought pops into my head and I start to laugh.

"Why are you laughing?" she asks.

"I'm just thinking about this friend of mine. He was with one of those religions that goes door to door. Super nice guy. I didn't care much for his views on a lot of things, but we got along just fine. Anyways,

I asked him once, out of all the doors he's knocked on, over all the years, how many people he brought into his church."

"How many?"

"Zero. Twenty plus years the guy never closed a single deal."

"That's funny?" she asks flatly.

"No, what's funny is what happened after. I asked him for the sales pitch and then spent the afternoon with him working on how he could improve it. I didn't care so much about the religious part; I took offence to the poor salesmanship. And I'm laughing because here I was giving him advice and I couldn't even arouse the slightest bit of spiritual curiosity in my own children. I know what to do. I'm just a little disappointed and I don't want to do it."

"What's that?" she asks.

Lo, Radiant one, I will tend to your garden with gentleness and care. I will war for you no longer, and I will dance, around the fire and beneath the stars. I will write for you. I will love you with my words. My buildings and creations will not be for my glory, but instead will be a testament to our love. I will light beacons so that your lost ones can find their way back to you. I will not wake them, not abruptly from their dream nor their nightmare, but I will point to the light that will guide the way back home.

"I need to learn how to dance."

"You hate dancing."

"Yup. That's why I'm disappointed."

I don't want to dance. Figuratively or literally. I just don't know how to explain what's happening inside me. Where my heart is pulling me. I could have said *I want to build an ark*. It's closer to how I feel and slightly less crazy than some of the other voices.

There are all kinds of voices inside me. The inner child. Inner rascals, sages, and the critics. The loudest one I hear right now, next to the nerd, is my inner revolutionary. The burning I feel. I want to be part of a revolution. I want to be part of the generation that restores this world to its fullest glory, that one that makes Life sacred once again.

My children were born in hospitals. Seconds after leaving the womb, they were wrapped in cotton and placed in plastic trays. They were rolled into a room with other infants and cooed and cried under fluorescent lighting. Their mother was drugged and slept. As for me, I wandered the mostly empty antiseptic concrete halls. Lonely. No bells sounded; no songs of praise were sung. There was no feast or celebration. This hallowed moment was dissected and emptied of all its beauty, because I did not sanctify it. I did not bless it or render it sacred. Kneeling with reverence, weeping with joy, singing songs of praise are no-nos where I come from. Best case, and only if it's a boy, a cigar with a few close friends.

I was beside my paternal grandfather when he drew his last breath.

That was a sacred moment that I carry with me to this day. I rubbed his hair and kissed his forehead in the seconds before his final exhale. But for my grandmother's funeral I was away, on an airplane, busy and preoccupied. And so many more moments of sanctity were forever lost to a blind pursuit of inconsequential power because I could not see what they were.

I grew up in a culture and era where very little was sacred. In our pursuit of freedom, we overreached; in our desire to free ourselves from the traditions of oppressive religion, we ran away from the heart of tradition and religious beauty itself. We gained sexual liberation but lost sensuality, that sacred dance between beauty and desire. In our conquering knowledge we have lost our innocence, our ability to look at the world with awe and wonder.

We have all but destroyed the churches and the temples, robbed ourselves of the profound beauty of shared worship. That's nobody's fault. But we have an opportunity to correct it. Only we, the truly free people of the twenty-first century, can make our world one of veneration and beauty. It is for us to celebrate the births and mourn the deaths together. For us to rejoice at the fall harvest and weep at the first spring flower. It is for us to rebuild the temples and sacred places, to share our worship—not of God, but of the unfolding beauty of creation. The profound beauty of us. Of me and of *you*. What is this story you are writing, this love you are seeking? What is this beauty you are creating? Your fears and anxieties are plain; I share them. Your connection to the divine might take a different path, but all streams come from the same source. The path away from the source, however... your path? Mystery.

Existence and consciousness are hard work. The duality of life—joy and suffering, confusion and enlightenment, love and loss, triumph and tragedy—none of this is for the weak. Your first act of conscious will, to leave the ultimate peace of the lotus flower, to venture into this world, paying the price of admission and forgetting your most basic awesome nature... *Why did you do that?*

You are the profound central mystery that sages throughout the span of time and across cultures have been celebrating. The temples, the traditions, the dances, the chants, the ancient scriptures, the sacred fires, and plant brew—they are for you. *It was always you.*

"Are you crying?" Nancy asks.

"No."

There might be a tear somewhere on my face that squeezed out accidently. *Baby, we are so close. We've come so far. There is a bridge, between heaven and earth, just over there...*

Whenever she wants to know what I'm really thinking she just looks into my eyes intensely. I usually get a little uncomfortable, but right now, I don't flinch. I look deeply into hers.

She smiles.

I don't know why she's smiling, but if she saw something she liked that's good enough for me.

CHAPTER 37 — SO MAKE YOURSELF AN ARK OF CYPRESS WOOD

Nancy is in the bedroom on a video call with Elliott and her parents. I can't hear what she is saying, but I can hear her laughing and the murmur of her voice. Just talking. They speak for over an hour.

I exchange a few texts with John, Stefano, and Duncan. All three are well. Coping with the various restrictions in the UK. A little like me, they are muddling along. No major life changes except in the way each spoke. There was a gentleness in the way they described the muddling. Stefano was thinking about changing jobs. John was busy helping neighbours, and Duncan was supporting his girlfriend through some career changes of her own.

Duncan is happy, and despite having only spent a few hours with him, his happiness makes me smile. That he and his girlfriend are pulling together against the forces of the world that want to pull them apart. Their struggle: my favourite kind of muddling.

\#

"I'm sorry, that went on longer than I thought," Nancy says as she comes into the kitchen.

"I love listening to you talk. I wish I had your skill," I say.

"Next time you are on the call with the kids, just let the silence speak and see what happens. Don't force it. It'll happen all by itself," she says.

We spent the weekend apartment hunting in Abu Dhabi. The cities have opened up from the quarantine. This storm hasn't fully passed and the mosques are still closed, but people are moving again.

Nancy's job will take us an hour up the road from Dubai. It is me following her career now. Her work life has been reinvigorated these past few months. I thought we would only be out here a couple of years, but Nancy is thinking long term. She focused so much of the last few years on motherhood, and now this is a chance for her to express herself professionally and a chance for me to experience the supporting rather than lead role.

#

It's late evening here, which means lunchtime back home. It's the weekend so a good chance the kids will just be getting up. I throw out a Zoom video call invite and before long I have three livestream videos playing on my phone.

Emma just dyed her hair—pink and red. Amelia has changed her background to a random picture from *The Simpsons*, and Jesse is still in bed. His eyes are a little droopy.

I initiate the transactions. One by one, I ask them how their week has been. What their plans for the summer will be. If they need anything, financial or Amazon delivery. It's mostly a one-way conversation. Short answers. Everyone is good but bored. They are still under strict quarantine in Canada.

Right now, they don't need anything. Amelia might take a pre-university course over the summer; she's thinking business and law. Emma is busy working. Jesse is caught off-guard by the girls' plans, so he makes something up. He has no plan and that's just fine. He'll figure this part out without my overbearing help, and I can cheer from the sidelines, for all of them.

The call goes silent. I just look at their faces. And it hits me. A dawning awareness and a new insight. A sense of my own transformation. True North. Why I am doing what I am doing.

"Dad, why are you smiling?" Amelia asks.

"You guys… You're just so beautiful," I tell them.

"So weird," Jesse says.

"Bye," Emma says.

"Love you, guys," I say.

"Love you too, Pops," they say.

Twenty years ago, when I called my mom to tell her Emma was born and I had become a father, she surprised me with a question: *Can you remember the world without her in it?* It was a strange question and the answer even more strange. No. I couldn't remember. Emma was barely a day old and I didn't remember ever not feeling like a father. Until this past year or so. I've been feeling something new. Seeing the kids over Zoom, coping so well without me, it hit me. What I'm feeling.

With my grandad gone and my dad not at full health, I didn't have someone I could bounce these feelings off, these changes.

I think I am becoming a grandfather.

The kids might not be planning a baby anytime soon, but something in me has changed. My drive. What I care about. I am not confused anymore.

Noah and the Ark. I think the point of the story gets a little lost in the details of what kind of wood he used to build the ark and exactly how many animals he brought on board. The point of the story, at least to me, is about a grandfather's love. If a father's drive is the well-being of his own children, a grandfather's drive is about the well-being of the children to come. The unborn generations ahead. Their families and the world they will inherit. The birds and the elephants.

It's about trying to protect and preserve all that is beautiful and sacred from the chaos of the world.

The children of my children. The health of their community and nation. The temples and the love of the mystics that inspired them. The shared values and practices that will enlighten their minds and expand their hearts. My drive is changing. I want to build an ark for the kids and their families. Maybe not so many animals, but the kids for sure.

The realization is making me smile. Not so much the ark and the flood part, but the part where I'm not losing my mind. That I'm not becoming a trustafarian or a nomad or a sadhu, just a new grandfather who cares about the well-being of the generations to come.

For once, I have no idea what I'm doing, but I know exactly why I'm doing it. There's a sense of peace in that feeling. That's enough for me today.

CHAPTER 38 — THE YUGA OF KALI

Time is a funny thing. When you break it down enough, it's just an abstract measurement of a rhythm of motion between two things. The dance between our planet and the sun; the moon's orbit, the oceans, the fertility and decay cycles of organic life here on Earth.

In time, my grandad passed away in 2014. The same year, scientists got a glimpse of one of the largest cosmic structures ever observed. A thread of the cosmic web stretching two million light years across the universe. A new working hypothesis emerged that, at large scales, our cosmos may resemble a spider's web. Everything that has ever happened and ever will happen, occurring along tiny filaments of a vast cosmic web.

This year, 2020, amidst the confusion and chaos here on Earth, quite literally the biggest news of the past twelve months is going mostly unreported. On May 19, 2019, the area around Sgr A*, the supermassive black hole at the centre of our home galaxy, got seventy-five times brighter. Nobody knows why or how. This is true. The supermassive black hole at the centre of our galaxy, four million times more massive than our sun, got seventy-five times brighter. Astronomers around the world shrugged in unison.

We also discovered a baby solar system: Beta Pictoris is an infant star and emerging system. Roughly twice the size of our sun, B-Pic is only twenty-ish million years old; our sun, earth, and moon, in contrast, are over 4.5 billion years old. There is still a large disk of dust and gas orbiting the star, along with planetesimal belts and cometary activity that astronomers believe are the building blocks for planets.

In our present era of science, we are generally predisposed toward thinking the underlying principle of the cosmos is chaos. Random collisions of atoms and genetic material. But it only looks that way when sliced apart. When we try and dissect the world into tiny moments and particles, caught between cycles and rhythms. If you aren't around long enough to see a seed germinate into a flower, all you can study is random and spontaneous occurrences of flowers.

There's a parable that I like about an old fish. The old fish swims by two young fish and says, "Hey, boys, how's the water?" One young fish looks to the other and says, "What the hell is water?"

We aren't big enough to see the intricate web of this universe. We don't live long enough to watch our galaxy birthing new stars, solar systems, and planets. But if a person can transcend time, even for just a moment and feel it all at once—leave the senses, the self, and the pressing needs of the day for just a minute or two and connect with everything that is, was, and ever will be—a new sense emerges.

It's all okay.

Rajesh tells me that long ago, deep in the Himalayan ranges, the ancient Hindus studied the stars. The old yogis charted the rhythms of the cosmos.

They started with the rotation of the planet, one solar day. Then the orbit of our planet around the sun, one solar year. They worked their way up to the orbit of our sun around the black hole at the centre of the galaxy; our galactic orbit, 230 million years. And then all the way up to a *kalpa*, the cycle of the creation and destruction of the universe. They considered this to be exactly one day long. *One day in the mind of God.*

The yogis divided this kalpa into four uneven segments. Four yugas: Satya, Treta, Dvapara, and this our present yuga—the Kali Yuga. The last and shortest. The yuga of acceleration. The yuga of conflict and strife.

And although *conflict and strife* might read as a rough deal, the yogis believed that the acceleration also means that it is a time of great awakening.

It's not impossible that we are living in the era of the Great Awakening. That this global pandemic will not be the opening chapter to decades of warfare like it was a century ago, but rather an entirely new book. A book where elephants walk the forests of Cambodia on four legs, not three.

Something else from the Hindu texts Rajesh has shared with me. The Bhagavad Gita.

I like the Hindu scripture because it's conversational. Dialogue. In the case of the Bhagavad Gita, it is a conversation between the warrior Arjuna and the Godhead Krishna.

In one section, Krishna imparts to Arjuna the three modes of nature. The way of goodness, passion, and ignorance.

"Sometimes the mode of passion becomes prominent, defeating the mode of goodness, O son of Bharata. And sometimes the mode of goodness defeats passion, and at other times the mode of ignorance defeats goodness and passion. In this way, there is always competition for supremacy."When you see there is nothing beyond these modes of nature in all activities and that the Supreme Lord is transcendental to all these modes, then you can know my spiritual nature."

I've had moments of transcendence. I'm also ignorant, passionate, and good. I'm a man, a human. Of this Earth. An ordinary poplar. A man-shaped tree in a crowded forest reaching for the sunlight. Circa 2020, the Yuga of Kali.

GIF of Hamster Waving Goodbye.

Afterword

Dubai – Spring 2021

In the Archer's hands, she allowed her bow to bend with gladness.

My mom passed away a few months ago. Unexpectedly but peacefully. It was a complicated moment. Pandemic, quarantines, time zones. I wasn't able to travel, and my family back home took care of all the arrangements. We held a digital service and made plans for a family road trip to bring her ashes to the UK when the world opens back up.

I heard somebody say once that grief is the apex of love. That it is only because you have been so profoundly touched by someone that it hurts so much when they are gone. Last week my girls lived a nice moment together and instinctively I tried sharing it with my mom over WhatsApp. I caught myself, looked up at the sky, and smiled. Through the tears, I smiled. I'm feeling the apex of my love for my dearly departed mom.

I share this because this book has its own interesting footnote in my life. I got to share an early draft with my mom. At first, she didn't much care for it. She thought the writing was a little clunky and maybe she was a little irked by my portrayal of her. That she was depicted as a bit frailer than she thought herself to be. She stopped talking to me for a while.

When we finally met up at her apartment in person, we spoke about it. She broke down. We hugged. It was a tender moment. In my own little world, it was a miracle because part of her healed that day. The part that can love freely and smile a little easier. She spent the last few months of her life living with kindness and gratitude. For her last Christmas, she baked, sent me pictures, called my dad, and spent Boxing Day with the grandkids. She left not long after the new year. In her bed, sometime in the middle of night, she quietly stepped out of a party that she started. She left knowing all whom she loved and cared for were healthy and happy.

I cherish that moment in my mom's apartment and all the loving moments in her life that followed it. They are treasures to me. Loving moments, the only kind of earthly treasure worth accumulating and holding on to. The kind of wealth that underlines for me the religious life now.

I used the word *religion* fairly loosely in this book. It wasn't until writing this Afterword that I looked up the definition.

Religion: noun—the belief in and worship of a superhuman controlling power, especially in a personal god or gods.

In that case, I've been using the word incorrectly. The definition I'd like to use is this:

Religion: that thing humans do together outside of culture, politics, industry, and science to connect with and explore their innermost self to enhance their relation to one another and the world they live in.

This book is about that kind of religion. I feel that in this era, religious failings have been well documented. Religious critique and sometimes ridicule are fairly common amongst my close friends and in my world of business and technology. Rituals and practices are mocked because they serve no discernible rational purpose in the world of power and production. I hope this changes. I hope the more scientifically minded will dig for a deeper understanding of the religious experience and the more religious-minded can reflect on some of the criticism. There is a bridge between the rational and the divine, and I think our next evolutionary leap will happen once we find it.

I was sitting at the kitchen table a couple of years ago when I came across Thoth's prophecy. It's an old text. It's a lament, a wise old man speaking to his student, foretelling the sad days to come about a world without religion.

O Egypt, Egypt, of thy religion nothing will remain but an empty tale, which thine own children in time will not believe. Nothing will be left but graven words and only the stones will tell of thy piety. And in that day, men will be weary of life and they will cease to think the universe worthy of reverent wonder and worship. And so religion, the greatest of all blessings, will be threatened with destruction; men will think it a burden and will come to scorn it. They will no longer love this world around us, this incomparable work of God, this glorious structure, this sum of all good made up of many diverse forms, this instrument whereby the will of God operates in that which he has made, ungrudgingly favouring man's welfare. This combination and accumulation of all the manifold things that can call forth for veneration, praise and love of the beholder.

I read Thoth's prophecy on the August 20, 2019. I know the exact day because it was the same day of the report on a Russian nuclear accident. It was a small accident. Nowhere near the scale of Chernobyl and got much less coverage. Speculation was around the testing of a new type of nuclear-powered missile referred to in the west as the SSC-X-9 Skyfall. The locomotive-size missile is meant to be able to fly almost indefinitely and circumvent modern antimissile defenses: a radioactive missile-train flying at treetop level.

We are living in a time where nuclear-powered missile accidents barely make the day's headlines. Antidepressants, suicides, wars, random acts of violence, the general pillaging of Earth and biosphere, and the lies, dear God, the lies, the constant stream of bullshit beamed real-time around the world. It is plain to see in the aggregate that these are symptoms of a deeper problem. I did not cause this problem; neither did anyone alive today. Ours is not a story of villains. It is, though, a story of passionate ignorance.

For a long time, I was ignorant. Callow and cretinous. My life had been a reaction to one thing or another. Had it not been for the grace, the goodness of loving strangers at a few key points in my life, I can say with certainty that at best I would be living in a loveless darkness. My life was an intensive pursuit of wealth and power, with equally intensive paroxysms of frustration and anger, waves of survival, pyrrhic victories, and cascading defeats. No beauty, no love—just blind pursuit of a strange kind of empty happiness.

I decided to give religion, all religion, another look. I decided to explore, with open eyes and heart, with the spirit of Herodotus, a kind of innocent curiosity. To move past the criticism, the injustices, and hypocrisy and focus only on the shared practices, the rituals, the attempts to free a person from the world, to reconnect with spirit, inspiration, and divinity. What I found, what I am finding still, is the striving. Toward goodness. Toward harmony. Within self and between selves, between the three modes of nature and the occasional, transcendent moment away from nature itself.

Our problems today, from climate change to social justice, generational disenfranchisement and oppression, war and peace, healthcare, education, and institutional reform are all complex, interlinked, and global. In the rational space, in the realm of logic, good and bad, left and right, the problems are intractable. Our children can point them out, scream in microphones, and our politicians can stand on podiums promising solutions. But political will, however noble, will not bring eight billion people into harmony with our shared ecosystem or put the nuclear genie back in the bottle.

Rational debate—you are wrong, I am right—works well enough when the problems are simple, but solving twenty-first-century problems demands a little more. That we seek unity over victory. Wisdom over knowledge. There aren't two sides to any issue anymore, and one-sided advocacy is little more than shrill. In the religious space, however, in the realm of spirit, in mystical exploration, the problems take on a different form. They become problems of unity, creativity, harmony, clarity, wisdom, and love.

Often, big problems don't require big solutions, only subtle shifts in imagination and a willingness to act. Not because of a Utopian ideal but simply because it's our most basic nature. It's who we are.

In the 1980s, a few grey whales were trapped under the ice in the Arctic near Alaska. A lone man with a chainsaw began cutting holes in the ice to let them breathe. Others joined him, and before long an international relief effort had been mobilized to save those whales. These whales were nothing special. They were ordinary and gray. They held no great value, and their survival didn't really matter, except to the man with the chainsaw. But within days, those whales mattered to the whole world. Their plight made front page headlines, and video of the effort was broadcast around the globe.

For what seemed like the first time in my life at that point, the Soviet Union and the United States were collaborating. Working together to save those whales. There was no economic reason behind it; it wasn't marketing, or a publicity stunt to increase brand value. It wasn't a considered diplomatic strategy to bring the countries together. It was just us in our most natural state, cooperating. Unity, harmony, love. Caring for Earth and all its inhabitants. Absent the world of the abstract and made-up things, we take care of the whales. We heal the sick and share our good fortune with those less fortunate. We put out the fires. We draw a line in the sand to shield the turtles from tourists and we build prosthetic feet for injured elephants.

The arc of nature in harmony bends toward goodness. And so do we.

True holy men and women still live among us, quietly busy, grounded in the daily work of nurturing and enlightening, of rendering little moments and corners of the world sacred. And there are the forest dwellers, the shamans. The ones who never forgot our true origin and purpose. The ones who never lost our original connection to Spirit, and who have kept the fire of wisdom burning; through them a new zeitgeist will emerge. A day of power and wisdom in balance. Desire and beauty in unity. Their voices are quiet now. Denied and dismissed, they speak softly, confident that truth needs no advocate. They transcend power and seek no followers. They live among us, healing, helping, revealing truth to those who wish to awaken to it.

And it is for them that I write: that I may lend my voice to theirs, in the hope of amplifying their truth, that my voice may become one of the many in the growing choir of humanity, singing in harmony toward a swirling cosmos, with joy, gratitude, and reverence at the birth of our new epoch.

I dedicate this book to them and to the man with the chainsaw who saw a pod of ordinary grey whales trapped in the ice and decided to cut a hole.

-AT

ABOUT THE AUTHOR

Alexander Thomas grew up in Canada and the UK but now lives
in Dubai. He writes from the perspective of a father, husband,
technology innovator and entrepreneur.

In his business life, Alex founded a global aviation technology
company that has taken him around the globe. These travels
have allowed him to explore cultures, religions, spiritual practices
and temples with a sense of wonder, appreciation and a deep
love of humanity.

Man in Motion is Alex's first book.

ABOUT THE PUBLISHER

The Dreamwork Collective is a print and digital publisher sharing diverse voices and powerful stories with the world. Dedicated to the advancement of humanity, we strive to create books that have a positive impact on people and on the planet. Our hope is that our books document this moment in time for future generations to enjoy and learn from, and that we play our part in ushering humanity into a new era of heightened creativity, connection, and compassion.

www.thedreamworkcollective.com

@thedreamworkcollective

CPSIA information can be obtained
at www.ICGtesting.com
Printed in the USA
BVHW071114201021
619391BV00005B/122